BFI Modern Classics

Rob White
Series Editor

BFI Modern Classics is a series of critical studies of films produced over the last three decades. An array of writers explore their chosen films, offering a range of perspectives on the dominant art and entertainment medium in contemporary culture. The series gathers together snapshots of our passion for and understanding of recent movies.

Forthcoming

City of Sadness
Berenice Reynaud

Dilwale Dulhaniya Le Jeyenge
Anupama Chopra

Heat
Nick James

The Idiots
John Rockwell

Jaws
Antonia Quirke

LA Confidential
Manohla Dargis

Stanley Kubrick with Nicole Kidman and Madison Egington on the set of *Eyes Wide Shut*
(*Stanley Kubrick: A Life in Pictures*, produced and directed by Jan Harlan,
© 2001 Warner Bros.)

Eyes Wide Shut

Michel Chion

Translated by
Trista Selous

 Publishing

First published in 2002 by the
British Film Institute
21 Stephen Street, London W1T 1LN

Copyright © Michel Chion 2002
Translation copyright © Trista Selous 2002
Reprinted 2005

The British Film Institute promotes greater
understanding and appreciation of,
and access to, film and moving image
culture in the UK.

British Library Cataloguing-in-Publication Data
A catalogue record for this book is available
from the British Library

ISBN 0-85170-932-X

Series design by Andrew Barron &
Collis Clements Associates

Typeset in Italian Garamond and Swiss 721BT
by D R Bungay Associates, Burghfield, Berks

Printed in Great Britain by
Cromwell Press, Trowbridge, Wiltshire

Contents

Acknowledgments

My thanks go first of all to Rob White, who suggested I should write this book. I should also like to thank Michel Ciment for all the information and encouragement he has given me, my students at the Ecole Supérieure d'Etudes Cinématographiques (ESEC) in Paris for our discussions, and my wife Anne-Marie for her support.

Where captions incorporate dialogue or scene directions, they are drawn from the screenplay of *Eyes Wide Shut*, published by Warner Books (1999).

Eyes Wide Shut

1. 'You're not even looking at it'

'You're not even looking at it,' says Alice to Bill. She has just asked if her hair looks all right and her husband has replied, 'It's great,' without looking at it. They are about to go out to a very smart party and she has done her hair in a magnificent cascade of curls.

But, at the point when she asks him, 'Is my hair OK?' she is just getting up from the toilet seat, where she has been sitting to urinate, wiping herself discreetly afterwards beneath her lifted dress and – it's true – whether out of indifference or a certain sense of decency, he hasn't looked at her.

'You're not even looking at it' could also be a warning addressed to the film's audience, and more still to the critic thinking of writing about the film. Although video and DVD enable him to keep all its images at home and see everything as often as he likes, he may still very easily fail to look in the right place at the right time.

After all this film is called *Eyes Wide Shut* and, just before the title appears on screen, we have seen Alice from behind, in a room, taking off an evening dress to appear naked. The image lasted no more than a few seconds, between two cuts. So viewers who have come with the intention of seeing and keeping their eyes wide open have briefly admired Nicole Kidman; they may

ALICE: You're not even looking at it

well have said to themselves that, if they were Bill Harford, Alice's husband, they would not have missed the chance to look at her.

The following evening Alice remembers the naval officer for whom she would have abandoned everything and identifies what triggered her desire: 'He glanced at me.'

In another scene from the film, during an erotic masked ball, another woman, completely naked but seen from the front – only her face is hidden by a mask – comes into a library with a man dressed in a cape and a Venetian mask. The next shot shows the same man from the same angle and in the same room, with the woman beside him, but both are shown at a little more distance. The woman goes up to Bill, who is also wearing a mask, and asks him to go with her to a more private place. For the cinema audience, this has to be the same woman.

Yet, if we watch the film again at home, we discover something rather strange: there is not one woman but two; or rather, the first woman is replaced by another from one shot to the next. They both wear the same mask and are with the same man (hence the confusion), but they do not have the same breasts (the second woman's are heavier) or the same pubic hair (the first woman's is more shaved). In the normal run of things every member of the audience might be expected to notice this; but to do so, they would all have to take a good look at the taboo body parts on display before their eyes, they would have to compare breasts and pubic hair. Perhaps the

'The man in the unicorn mask enters the room accompanied by a naked young woman'

YOUNG WOMAN: Have you been enjoying yourself?

spectators are ashamed to look at what is shown to them; they don't always dare to really see what they're watching: 'You're not even looking at it.'

My aim here is to try to see what should be seen and to hear what should be heard; yet perhaps, inevitably, like the policemen in Edgar Allan Poe's story 'The Purloined Letter', who go to the place where the letter has been hidden but do not notice it lying there before their eyes, we shall neither see nor hear anything.

Or perhaps the film would say that both seeing and hearing are an illusion.

2. 'Do you feel like playing?'

Eyes Wide Shut is Kubrick's last and, in my view, one of his three greatest films, alongside *2001: A Space Odyssey* (1968) and *Barry Lyndon* (1975). It's the story of a young doctor and his wife, Bill and Alice Harford, who live in Manhattan and have a daughter of about six or seven called Helena. One evening, during a pre-Christmas party given by the millionaire Ziegler, each has the chance to be unfaithful to the other, she with an attractive man of around fifty, he with two models; but nothing happens. The following evening they discuss the party and talk about how men and women experience jealousy. Probably to make her over-confident husband jealous, Alice tells him that she once almost left both him and their daughter for a naval officer. Bill seems devastated. Their conversation is interrupted when

Bill is called out because one of his patients has died. That night, while walking in south Manhattan, obsessed by the image of his wife giving herself to a stranger, he has further opportunities to be unfaithful to her: with the dead man's daughter, Marion, who tells him she loves him (but they are interrupted by her fiancé Carl); with a prostitute, Domino, who takes him home with her (but his wife calls him on his mobile phone and he decides to leave); lastly when, his identity concealed by a mask and cape, he goes to a secret meeting of the very rich. This is a ritualised orgy whose password he has been given by Nick Nightingale, a former fellow student turned jazz pianist. To find a costume to rent at such a late hour, Bill has had to wake Milich, a most peculiar individual. While serving Bill, Milich catches his daughter of about fifteen in her underwear with two Japanese gentlemen, whom he locks up in his shop. This girl also gives Bill an inviting glance.

In the grand mansion outside New York, where the orgy is taking place, Bill is soon identified as not belonging to that world, although, like everyone else, he is wearing a mask. One of the women from the orgy begs him to leave, saying, 'It could cost me my life and possibly yours'. When Bill appears before the assembled participants, it seems he may be about to suffer an unpleasant fate; however the same woman makes a theatrical offer to redeem him by suffering we know not what punishment in his stead. He has to leave, without knowing what is going to happen to the woman.

On returning home, Bill finds Alice laughing in her sleep. She is having a nightmare, which she describes to him when she wakes up. In this dream Alice was taking part in an orgy and laughing at her husband, who was also present. Bill tells her nothing of his own night's experiences.

The following day Bill tries to get back to his interrupted adventures of the previous night. However it is Carl rather than Marion who answers the phone. Domino, with whom he almost had sex, is not at home; she has discovered that she is HIV-positive. When Bill returns in daylight to the mansion where the orgy took place, he is handed a letter warning him to abandon his enquiries. Afterwards, when he takes his costume back to the shop (all except the mask, which he has lost), Milich's behaviour has changed completely; he very clearly gives Bill to understand that he is offering him his 'daughter''s sexual services.

Ziegler's party: a 'curtain of light'

The orgy at Somerton

Alice recounts her dream: 'hundreds of men, everywhere'

MILICH: Anything again – *anything* at all

Bill also learns that Nightingale has been abducted from his hotel by two men, who may also have beaten him up, and has left the city. Then he discovers that a former beauty queen named Amanda Curran, possibly the woman who offered herself as a victim in order to save him, has suffered an overdose. She has died and he goes to see her at the morgue. Is this the woman whose bad reaction to drugs he previously treated during the party hosted by Ziegler (who was sleeping with her)? Bill receives a call from Ziegler, who wants to talk to him.

At Ziegler's there is a long discussion: the millionaire says that he was present at the orgy, that he saw everything, that the house was full of very important people and that Bill should not get involved. He also tells him, but not immediately, that Amanda's sacrifice was staged to get rid of Bill, and that she was not killed; according to Ziegler it was her own fault that she died of an overdose; it was because of the life she was living and had nothing to do with the orgy. Bill's belief that she had been murdered was just his imagination running away with him.

Bill goes home, once again at night. His wife is sleeping in the marital bed and, next to her on the pillow, in her husband's place, lies the mask that he was wearing during the orgy. Bill cracks: 'I'll tell you everything,' he sobs. This is followed by an ellipsis. Later, in the small hours, we see them crying together. Life returns to normal and husband and wife are talking in a toy shop decorated for Christmas, where they have gone to buy presents with their daughter. Alice tells her repentant husband that they should be grateful that they have survived all their 'adventures', real or dreamed, that she loves him, that they are both now 'awake' – 'hopefully for a long time to come', and that the one thing they must do as soon as possible is 'fuck'. Cut to the final credits.

The above is a brief résumé, with no attempts at interpretation or understanding the characters 'from within', of the strange story Kubrick chose to tell in what was sadly to be his last film. It is a story set in the present day, but taken from a short story written in German in 1925 by the Viennese author Arthur Schnitzler. Kubrick had long wanted to adapt this story and remains extraordinarily faithful to its narrative thread.

Schnitzler has often been described as a 'Freudian' writer because of the presence of dreams in his work, not to mention the fact that both he and the inventor of psychoanalysis lived in the same city at the same time. There is even a famous letter of Freud's, dated 14 May 1922, in which he praises Schnitzler, saying that the reason he has never been to see him is that he is afraid of meeting 'his double'.

Schnitzler spent a long time thinking about his *Traumnovelle* ('Dream Story').[1] He wrote it when he was sixty-three years old, which was also Kubrick's age when he began work on the film. It is an

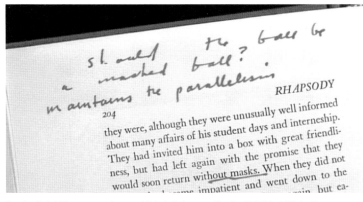

Stanley Kubrick's annotated copy of Schnitzler's story (*Stanley Kubrick: A Life in Pictures*, produced and directed by Jan Harlan, © 2001 Warner Bros.)

extraordinarily rich piece of writing, a real challenge for any film-maker, partly because of the images of the orgy, but also because what does not happen is much more important than what does.

So what is this story about? Why was Kubrick drawn to it?

3. 'It's only a dream'

Twenty-four dark slaves were rowing the magnificent galley that was to carry Prince Amgiad to the Caliph's palace. But the Prince, dressed in his crimson mantle, lay alone on the bridge beneath the dark blue night sky, scattered with stars, and his gaze …

We shall never know what the splendid prince was looking at, since the writer who gave us these lines, borrowed from the cycle of *The Thousand and One Nights*, immediately goes on, 'Until that moment the little girl had been reading aloud and now, almost at once, her eyes closed. Her parents looked at each other with a smile [*Bisher hatte die Kleine laut gelesen, beinahe plötzlich fielen ihr die Augen zu*].'

So this is how the *Traumnovelle* begins, with reading aloud followed by sleep, in which the story perhaps becomes a dream. The story being read transports us to a nocturnal, fantastical setting, which is suddenly brutally interrupted by the word 'gaze' (*Blick*) at the most exciting point

HELENA: Before I jump into my bed

(perhaps the moment when the Prince's gaze will rest on the heroine), because the little girl who was reading has fallen asleep. In the film Helena does not read any magical tales (she wants to watch *The Nutcracker* on television and learns to read from a text devoid of any fantastical dimension);[2] as we have seen, the film begins with her parents.

However fidelity may take unexpected paths: for example, although the reading of this story is not literally included in the screen adaptation, its echoes are present everywhere.

Schnitzler's story makes several mentions of words that are not spoken: a sentence is interrupted at the beginning, while at the end Albertine prevents her husband from saying the word 'forever' (*immer*). At first sight *Eyes Wide Shut* does the opposite: Bill says the word 'forever' loudly and clearly; the inhibited Marion declares 'I love you', while Marianne, her prototype in Schnitzler's story, doesn't say it so clearly. However these spoken words are replaced by others that are unspoken, as we shall see.

Meanwhile two colours mentioned in the story the little girl is reading, the red of the prince's coat and the blue of the sky, are to be found everywhere in the film. Although the action unfolds mainly in contemporary Manhattan, the context of Christmas offers a pretext to include a great many decorative lights, while fairytale colours can be seen everywhere, with blue playing a particularly important role (the Harford's

Bill and Milich's daughter in the Rainbow boutique

bathroom and bedroom). This is also a film in which characters continue in their dreams actions they have begun 'out loud' (Alice's dream).

The little girl's eyes close, remaining mentally open to the vision of a magical prince created by words in a book. However, in the film the eyes closed over a vision are also those of a dead woman, whose half-closed eyelids no longer allow any glances to pass through; they are also the eyes of an inner dream pursued by someone who is awake and telling a story. As Alice – who is short-sighted – is talking about the possibly imaginary man she could have followed in her husband's place, she sometimes looks away, into herself, at a vision she alone can see and which the film will never enable us to share.

4. 'Would you like to come inside with me?'

According to Christiane Kubrick and Jan Harlan,[3] the idea of basing a film on the *Traumnovelle* first emerged in 1968, when *2001* was released. Kubrick had of course read the story in an English translation, entitled *Rhapsody*.[4] He optioned the book around 1970 and, when the option expired, definitively bought the adaptation rights.

At first Kubrick was thinking in terms of a 'period movie' transposed to London or even Dublin (to the society described by James Joyce's short story 'The Dead'). But on reflection he decided to bring it up to date and to set it in New York, the multicultural city of his childhood. This was a surprising and risky choice, since such a story of marital fidelity would inevitably be described as outdated. In reality the film makes a gamble on the perennial nature of certain problems, and indeed on their new currency in the light of recent advances in biology and medicine. According to Christiane Kubrick, the director had read a great many books on ethnology, which state that 'the most important question for a man is that of his paternity, of learning that his children are not his own'.[5]

After the release of *Full Metal Jacket* (1987), Kubrick worked energetically on two projects, before deciding to shoot *Eyes Wide Shut*; these were *A.I.* (ultimately offered to Steven Spielberg and released in 2001) and *Aryan Papers*, dealing with an episode from the Holocaust. It is

Jude Law and Haley
Joel Osment in Steven
Spielberg's *A.I.*

not significant for us that *A.I.* uses the genre of science fiction to deal with the myth of the male child, the desire for a male child. In my personal interpretation, *Eyes Wide Shut* is told from the point of view of a male individual conceived in a sexual act between the two main characters which takes place after the end of the film.[6]

Kubrick began looking for a co-writer to work with him on the script and chose Frederic Raphael.

Raphael is an American who has lived mostly in 'Europe', as the Americans say, which in his case means, like Kubrick, in England. He is a cultivated man, familiar with the history and literature of antiquity. As well as the scripts of *Two for the Road* (Stanley Donen, 1966, with Albert Finney and Audrey Hepburn) and *Darling* (John Schlesinger, 1966, with Julie Christie), he has written a dozen novels, some biographies and essays, and has worked collaboratively on translations from Ancient Greek and Latin.

Our main source of information for the scriptwriting phases is Raphael's book *Eyes Wide Open*, which came out at the same time as the film.[7] This is a source to be used with caution. The title somewhat treacherously suggests that Raphael clearly saw things that Kubrick did not, or at least not all by himself. However the veracity of this book, in which details of conversations between Kubrick and his co-writer are ostensibly recorded, is disputed by the dead director's wife and brother-in-law, Christiane Kubrick and Jan Harlan.

5. 'What were you dreaming?'

Kubrick and Raphael's adaptation of the story was both very faithful
(some of the dialogue is unchanged) and very free, notably with the
addition of the character of Ziegler.

For example, at the beginning of Schnitzler's story, when the little
girl has gone to sleep, her parents, Albertine (who becomes Alice in the
film) and Fridolin (who becomes Bill) discuss the events of the previous
night in the evening quiet of their apartment. Their conversation
describing their night at the carnival is summed up using the past tense.
Each of them has flirted with other people, without consequences on
either side. The film locates the ball at the home of the millionaire Ziegler
and makes it the start of the action. The bitter-sweet discussion between
husband and wife, which opens Schnitzler's story, does not take place until
the following day, after the characters' daily routine has been shown.

Right from his opening pages, Schnitzler creates a charming
atmosphere of family life and *Gemütlichkeit*,[8] an ironic contrast to the
sexual adventures described. In conveying the conversation between the
two characters, he uses a phrase that sets the tone for the whole of
Kubrick's film and indicates the mix of complicity and distrust between
the couple: 'Innocent yet crafty questions and sly answers with double
meanings went back and forth [*Harmlose und doch lauernde Fragen,
Verschmizte, doppeldeutige Antworten wechselten hin und her*].'

In Schnitzler's story, Fridolin responds to Albertine's 'confession' of
her dreams of an affair with a naval officer by recounting a similar daydream
about a girl, which he had during the same holiday. This story is not told in the
film, which abandons symmetry and makes the doctor into a character who
confides nothing of himself; on the other hand the temptation represented by
a very young girl returns in the character of Milich's daughter.

Fridolin returns to the city in a locked carriage with opaque
windows. His journey is full of incidents apparently well-suited to the
cinema; yet Kubrick prefers to drop all this 'action' and to cut directly
from the shot in the big house, where his hero receives the order to leave,
to another showing him opening the door to his apartment, dressed once
more in ordinary clothes.

On his way home Schnitzler's Fridolin reflects on what he has seen. The questions he ponders – were the girls all prostitutes hired to play a part and was the whole thing just an act? – are posed in the film only in the explanatory scene and then by Ziegler not Bill.

Schnitzler's story ends with dialogue that returns in the film, with the proviso that Kubrick moved the setting of the couple's last conversation to a toy shop, whereas Schnitzler sets it in the bedroom.

When Fridolin asks, 'What should we do? [*Was sollen wir tun?*]' Schnitzler has Albertine answer, 'with a slight hesitation': 'Be grateful to Fate … that we have safely come through all these adventures, both real and dreamed [*Dem Schicksal dankbar sein, … dass wir aus allen Abenteuern heil davondekommen sind – aus dem wirklichen und aus den geträumten*].' The film takes out the reference to 'Fate', along with all other references to providence or destiny; only the word 'grateful' remains.

When Albertine says that both have now been woken and will remain awake for a long time: '"Forever," he wanted to add, but before he had uttered the words she laid a finger on his lips and, as though to herself, whispered, "Never question the future." [*Für immer, wollte er hinzufügen, aber noch ehe die Worte ausgesprochen, legte sie ihm einen Finger auf die Lippen und, wir vor sich hin, flüsterte sie: "Niemals in die Zunkunft fragen".*]'

As we know, in the film Bill does utter the word 'forever' – in fact he says it twice, as though tempting fate; on the other hand it is Sandor

'[Alice] kisses her index finger and plants it on Szavost's lips'

Szavost whom Alice silences by placing a finger on his lips, as though to establish a secret between them.

Schnitzler ends his story with a few fine, simple words of renewal: a new day is dawning and the sounds of life are heard again, including a child's clear laughter (*Kinderlachen*); of course the child is probably their own daughter, but it could also be a new child.

Having read the *Traumnovelle*, Raphael does not seem to have become its greatest fan, finding it 'a little bit … dusty'. He was particularly bothered by the length and extravagant visual detail of the dream narratives; of course at that stage he might have thought Kubrick was planning to film them.

They soon hit on the idea of beginning with the great 'showy Christmas binge', in the course of which the host has an erotic adventure while his wife is receiving the guests, and in which he also calls on the doctor's skills.

After this Raphael and Kubrick discussed how to add incident to the story. Raphael suggested that one solution might be to give the whole thing a dreamlike quality, but Kubrick insisted that the hero's fantasies and the heroine's dreams should be clearly distinguished from reality: 'If there's no reality, there's no movie.'[9] In practice no image in the film is ambiguous from this point of view: Bill's fantasies are visualised in black-and-white images (without dialogue); Alice's fantasy about the naval officer in Cape Cod and her dream of fornication are told in her own words with no accompanying images, although the addition of images, which cinema makes possible, might have lent them a certain reality.[10] This is an example of what might be called the refusal of any complicity or power-relation between image and speech; the latter does not give rise to images (except indirectly) and the former gives no visible confirmation of what is recounted.

One of Kubrick's earliest demands from his co-writer was 'no wit', nothing resembling a duo out of a romantic comedy, such as those made by Lubitsch, Cukor or, later, Stanley Donen; Kubrick criticised Raphael's first draft of the scene between Bill and the prostitute from this point of view, finding the dialogue too 'kinda boom-boom and a boom-boom'.[11]

There was another point on which Raphael says Kubrick had very fixed ideas: 'Transferring the story to New York seemed to me to offer an opportunity for keeping the Jewish aspect of the story, however it might be modernized. Kubrick was firmly opposed to it; he wanted Fridolin to be a Harrison Fordish goy and forbade any reference to Jews. ... In the end, Fridolin was to be given the surname Harford.'[12] Which, as Raphael notes, evokes the name Harrison Ford.

According to Jan Harlan, the introduction of the character of Ziegler – the script's main innovation – arose from Kubrick's desire to make a character from Bill's everyday life provide a link with the secret society of the participants at the orgy.

Ziegler unquestionably belongs to the family of provocative, shocking and libidinous father figures, at once both highly intelligent and extremely base, that are to be found throughout Kubrick's work. Examples include Adolphe Menjou's role in *Paths of Glory* (1957), Lee Ermey in *Full Metal Jacket*, Peter Sellers in *Lolita* (1961) and of course James Mason as the incestuous 'step-father' in the same film, and Jack Nicholson in *The Shining* (1980).

Various films served as reference points for Kubrick and Raphael while they were writing the script: Kieślowski's *Decalogue* cycle (1988 – which presents moral problems in allegorical form), Woody Allen's *Husbands and Wives* (1992) and Quentin Tarantino's *Pulp Fiction* (1994), which Kubrick advised Raphael to draw on, having been impressed by its pace.[13]

There was also the matter of what the film should be called, since it seems there was never any question of using the title of the original story, or its English version *Rhapsody*. It was Kubrick who suggested and insisted on *Eyes Wide Shut*. This title is an oxymoron (like *A Clockwork Orange*, 1971, from the book by Anthony Burgess and, to a certain extent, *Full Metal Jacket*) and retains an allusion to the original title in hidden form, since a dreamer's eyes are at once both open and shut.

6. 'What do I think? I dunno'

The story of the film adaptation is one of challenges. The task was to translate to the cinema something unshowable, something too dense and seemingly inaccessible to cinema. Film-makers have often sought to bring to the screen writers regarded as impossible to adapt, such as Marcel Proust (Schlöndorff, Ruiz),[14] Malcolm Lowry and Herman Melville (Huston), William Burroughs (Cronenberg) and so on.

Schnitzler's story represents the same kind of challenge for the cinema, containing as it does phrases such as, 'he was more struck than surprised [*Er war mehr ergriffen als erstaunt*]', 'he felt lost [*Er fühlte sich wie erlöst*]' and 'he laughed again and did not recognise his own laughter [*Er lachte wieder und kannte sein Lachen nicht*]'.

In addition Schnitzler sometimes lingers for several pages on the hero's private thoughts, emotions and deliberations. There are several solutions open to an adapter faced with the classic problem of transposing what is regarded as a character's 'inner life' to the screen:

- The visualisation of thoughts, frequently employed by silent cinema, which shows us, sometimes metaphorically, what the character is thinking. This is the method used by Kubrick in the black-and-white images of Alice with the naval officer.
- The character's inner voice or simultaneous mental verbalisation, telling us what the person is thinking without their lips moving; this may also cover cases in which characters are heard and seen talking aloud to themselves. There are no examples of this method in *Eyes Wide Shut*.

Phantasms in black and white: Alice and the Naval Officer

- Phrases, images, sounds or melodies that the character has seen or heard, and which we have also seen or heard, which then recur 'in the mind' of the character. Kubrick does use this method. We twice hear repetitions of phrases that Bill has heard, surrounded by echoes, as though he were recalling them. These are women's voices in a man's head.

- Verbalisation after the event by a narrator who is outside the action, or by characters themselves ('he/she thought that', 'I felt … ') There is nothing of the kind in this script.

- The creation of circumstances intended to make characters externalise their emotions. For example, someone encountering a material difficulty (a door that is hard to open, a lighter that will not light, the character drops something) will 'overreact', 'betraying' their inner state in their excessive irritation. Alternatively characters may unconsciously use an object to interpret their thoughts (Marlon Brando playing with Eva Marie Saint's gloves when he is sexually attracted to her in *On the Waterfront,* 1954, Albert Finney greedily eating in front of a woman in *Tom Jones*, 1963). Kubrick does not employ this very widely used method. In *Eyes Wide Shut* all objects – every lift, every telephone – work, perfectly; taxi drivers take you to your destination and everyone does their job properly, right down to the humblest nurse or the desk clerk at the Hotel Jason. So the protagonists have no excuse or motive to attribute their problems to the external world, or to project their lack of satisfaction onto it, and no physical 'mediator' (object, animal) that can express their troubled state. Nor is there any rain, snowfall or sudden storm when their feelings reach their highest pitch of intensity. The world goes on turning in the same old way.

The symbolic and 'psychological' use of objects is another method scorned by Kubrick: Alice does not play nervously with her wedding ring or her glasses. Apart from 'forgetting' the mask (and here we do not know exactly when this happened), the characters do not make any Freudian slips.

So, from the range available, Kubrick rejects all the 'indirect' methods, those that create complicity and resonance between the inner world of the characters and the objective world; on the other hand, when necessary he does use the more direct, literal and 'naive' methods.

The mental images attributed to Bill that show his wife making love with another man are very clearly located in his head by the editing codes (alternating between Bill in colour in a taxi or in his office and the black-and-white image of his naked wife giving herself to a man whose face is not seen in detail, returning to Bill in a taxi or his office, in colour). We should note that they tell us nothing of the precise nature of the disturbing feelings they produce in Bill. *Eyes Wide Shut* is a film clearly detached from any form of 'subjectivism'; it is a film in which there is an objective world (even a mental image is an 'object'), and no one, neither in the audience or among the characters, can claim to be able to get inside the head of anyone else.

Speech is often used in films to express what is going on 'inside' a character, whether directly (they are supposed to be speaking their true feelings) or indirectly (they are clearly supposed to be lying). In Kubrick's last film the question is not posed in these terms: the dialogue has a concrete, objective existence. When we hear the words we can never assume that their meaning is entirely transparent, or that they are clearly concealing some precise meaning that is different from what they say. This feeling concurs with Kubrick's way of illuminating the activity of talking in itself, as an action in itself, which takes characters over and does not allow them to do anything else.

In *Eyes Wide Shut,* as in most of Kubrick's films, there are indeed a great many scenes in which people who are talking do not do anything else at the same time, such as walking, driving a car or carrying out some household task. Kubrick rarely interrupts a speech to introduce some realistic element, to 'let in some air'. Besides the obvious examples of the long and important conversations between husband and wife, in which they are totally focused on each other, and the big scene with Ziegler, we need only look at the conversation with the desk clerk at the Hotel Jason. The dialogue with Nightingale in the Sonata Café is interrupted only by a telephone call, which is itself part of the action.

So interruptions in a conversation are all decisive: these include the moment when the telephone rings and interrupts the scene between Alice and her husband, or when a serious-looking man comes asking for Nick (at Ziegler's) or Bill; each time we wonder what is going to happen.

Many have noted the 'banality' of the dialogue: the exchange of polite greetings: 'Thank you', 'Hello, how are you?', 'Merry Christmas, how nice to see you', 'This way, sir'. These phrases, heard throughout the film, are not platitudes to tell us that the characters are flat, but real phrases, as they are spoken in reality. Kubrick's singularity is that he films both phrases of this kind that have no obvious importance and phrases regarded as important (Alice's story) with such great care, and has his actors speak them with such precision. He brings the same meticulousness to bear on filming the act of opening a door and, a few seconds later, of passing a hand across a dead man's face. By always paying the same degree of attention to the act of listening and looking, no matter what it is that we see or hear, Kubrick gives us a different perspective on existence. The film does not impose on us a hierarchy of what is important and what is not.

7. 'Suppose I said all of that was staged'

As with all Kubrick's films after *2001*, *Eyes Wide Shut* was shot almost entirely in England. According to Jan Harlan, Kubrick initially planned to shoot the New York exteriors in London's East End, at night, with a few American phone boxes. However the conditions necessary for filming (including the need to close off streets) would have made this difficult and costly, so sets of parts of street exteriors were built. Martin Scorsese notes that the streets of the Village through which Bill wanders bear imaginary names (such as 'Wren St.') and do not quite 'resemble' the streets of New York.[15]

The interior scenes were shot at Pinewood Studios, with a few hospital scenes in and around London. Bill and Alice's apartment was based on the one where Kubrick lived with his wife in Manhattan in the early 1960s.

Kubrick liked Tom Cruise's work, particularly his performance in Oliver Stone's film *Born on the Fourth of July* (1989). The role of Bill is

ALICE: Any little fantasies about what handsome Doctor Bill's dickie might be like?

NICK: Hey, man! I just play the piano

Bill is warned off outside the Somerton mansion

very weighty, as he is in almost every scene (apart from the scene between Alice and Szavost) and, in the documentary *Stanley Kubrick: A Life in Pictures*, Cruise explains how difficult it was for him to play a role that went against his own personality: Bill Harford gives little away and observes a great deal; he remains impenetrable to the end, without the robust physique of a taciturn hero. Moreover he reflects an introverted type of man familiar in Kubrick's work and already seen at the core of such films as *2001: A Space Odyssey* (the 'transparent' role of Dave Bowman played by Keir Dullea), *Barry Lyndon* (Ryan O'Neal) and *Full Metal Jacket* (the 'Joker' played by Matthew Modine). This type of character contrasts with the readily clownish extroverts seen in some of Kubrick's other films and played by James Mason, Jack Nicholson or Peter Sellers. We can say without hesitation that, for a film that took so long to shoot, Tom Cruise's performance has a homogeneity, a clarity and rigour that are all the more worthy of admiration because his character is constantly in a position to seem ridiculous in the eyes of the audience.

Nicole Kidman's role is much shorter than that of her then husband, but it is very exposed since, with the story of the naval officer and that of her dream, she has two important monologues. She is dazzling in the film, and also fills the first – and sadly the last – great role for a young woman in Kubrick's work (that of Marisa Berenson in *Barry Lyndon* being almost silent).

The actors' accounts agree on the fact that, on the set of *Eyes Wide Shut*, Kubrick was both perpetually demanding and very flexible, curious to see all the possibilities, including those suggested by the actors. Nothing, says Nicole Kidman, was 'right' or 'wrong'. The director did not want a 'naturalistic' performance; he wanted something different, something special, something 'magical', sometimes bordering on caricature, but no more than bordering. Nicole Kidman's little high laughs in the early scene at home, Sidney Pollack's nervous playing with a billiard ball in the big male duet at the end, a particular hand gesture made by Todd Field in the scene at the Sonata Café ('Hey, man! I just play the piano') and the way that the desk clerk strokes his hair are among these touches, which stand out because they do not seem solely intended to externalise a character's inner state. *Eyes Wide Shut* is both the best-acted film in Kubrick's work and one of the best-acted films in the entire history of cinema, in which each actor finds the right, discreet nuances at any moment.

Kubrick also did everything to prevent his actors feeling the pressure of time, of a concept or a release date. Besides, shooting took such a long time, with a small crew and soft lighting, that by the end they were no longer aware of the cameras.

Kubrick's technique involved using a very small crew, often only six or seven people on set, which considerably reduced the cost of a day's shooting. This is reminiscent of Charlie Chaplin making and writing *City Lights* (1931), groping his way forward as he was filming, as shown in Kevin Brownlow's documentaries.

Pollack has given a humorous account of his participation in *Eyes Wide Shut*, and particularly the 'billiard room' scene, which was inspired by the long explanatory scenes in the *Columbo* series and was continually rewritten: 'We spent hours trying to find out what the characters knew and didn't know, what did and didn't need to be said.'[16] Kubrick encouraged Pollack to give him a theatrical performance and decided that the character should have sudden outbursts of vulgarity (Ziegler is the only character in the film to use the words 'cocksucker', 'prick' and 'asshole'). The character is as ambiguous as the one played by Peter Sellers in *Lolita*, but Pollack's solid, reassuring physique gives his character an ambiguity of a quite different, much deeper nature.

In relation to the image, Kubrick adapted techniques he had tried out in his previous work, using low lighting for everything and 'pushing' the film during development, resulting in a slight effect of graininess. As in several of his other films, almost everything is lit by the lights we see in the image, particularly since the Christmas context made it possible to use a great number of small bulbs. In *Eyes Wide Shut* Kubrick succeeds in creating images that are at the same time both cosmic and very intimate, in which the blue that reigns in a bedroom or bathroom opens up an enchanted space.

The camera style in *Eyes Wide Shut* is extremely varied, alternating a classic editing structure of shot/reverse shot (which is capable of infinite resources and is to film-makers what the scale is to a classical composer) and very flexible, wide angle tracking shots, particularly using Steadicam. Here again we see typical Kubrick tracking shots in which the character seems to take possession of a place just by walking down a corridor; these are executed with such great intensity that what, in the work of other directors, would be simple transition shots (going from one place to another), here to constitute the main action. This is why we shall give such importance to the tracking shot in which Marion's fiancé Carl walks, as Bill has done, from the door of the Nathanson apartment to the dead man's bedroom.

For some exterior shots, Kubrick sent a second unit and assistant set designer to New York, following his usual practice.

Then it was time to begin the editing and to select the music.

8. 'Would you like a table or would you like to sit at the bar?'

From the point of view of its shooting and editing, *Eyes Wide Shut* is not trying to be an ostentatiously well-shot film: the camera turning around Sandor and Alice as they dance at the beginning, or the circular tracking shots around the ring of women at the orgy ceremony are unobtrusive compared to what we see in most contemporary films. What singles them out is the precision and clarity with which they are executed. Kubrick remains faithful to the wide angle in many shots, and sometimes uses 180 degree reverse angles when filming a pair of characters from a new direction (the beginning of the scene inside the Rainbow boutique).

Kubrick's camera placement, framing and editing are also very precise. For example, Sandor Szavost, the suave Hungarian who keeps trying to get Alice upstairs, is not in any shot that does not also contain Alice. No shot gives him existence independently of her and, when she leaves him, he ceases to exist for us.

In some cases a character gains independence and existence after a little while: this is true of the prostitute Domino, who is initially seen only in wide and medium shots, in which Bill also figures. After he moves away from her to answer his wife's telephone call, she is the subject of a separate shot and begins to exist for us as a character independent of him.

Conversely, Marion very quickly becomes the subject of close-ups which linger on her face, linked to the serious atmosphere of this separate shot. Often – but not systematically – the scenes filmed in wide shots are given a lighter tone (in Milich's shop, the early part of the scene with Domino and Sally), whereas those that give an important place to close-ups are the more serious or disturbing scenes. The orgy in the big house, filmed in wide shots, is a special case, since everything that Bill sees seems to be choreographed for an audience.

The confrontations between husband and wife are of course very interesting to look at in terms of the shooting and editing structure. In the big scene of conjugal 'truth', Alice is the mobile element and Bill the fixed

ALICE: Millions of years of evolution, right? *Right?*

The reverse shot of Bill, as he takes in Alice's revelations

point: the editing gives Alice a dominant place and it is she who is seen the most. The camera follows her various postures – standing, seated, bending over, kneeling – and stops on her face when she starts to recount the episode in Cape Cod. The reverse shots of Bill, when he has stopped talking and is sitting frozen on the bed as he takes in these revelations, are at once short and extraordinary. Kubrick had long been trying to capture something on a face that was undergoing a transformation from within, a face that was changing. He sometimes obtained what he wanted through clowning and grimaces (Vincent d'Onofrio in *Full Metal Jacket*, Nicholson in *The Shining*), or through horror (*Full Metal Jacket*, again), but here it is a matter of a simple domestic argument.

Bill is accosted by Domino at night

Bill and the waitress at Gillespie's coffee shop

Most of the scenes in the film group the characters in pairs. The shooting and editing solutions adopted by Kubrick were simple: either the two characters are together in the same shot, or they are facing each other, in which case Kubrick generally uses a shot/reverse shot sequence, almost continuously avoiding symmetry (in other words using the same scale of frame for each character), by framing one of the characters more tightly.

Between the two characters there is often an object which acts as both an obstacle and a connection, such as the lamp between Bill and Marion, the lamp in the shape of a luminous ball between Bill and Nick, the bar between Bill and the waitress at Gillespie's and the counter between Bill and the gay desk clerk. The image may emphasise this object or it may not show it, with the effect of bringing the characters closer together.

Bill and Alice are brought together in the images of the opening scenes (which are dominated by shots in which they are both shown at once), before being separated by the action. They are again brought together in the images showing them caressing in front of the mirror, before being separated once again by the action (the montage sequence of their daily routine). Lastly they are separated by the editing during the great 'explanation' of the second evening: in fact from the moment when Alice moves away from the bed and her husband's body, she is no longer with him in any way, in any shot, right to the end of this long scene: the visual structure keeps them apart until the very end. It is the last image of the film that brings them together: she is seen from the front and he from behind in a shared image that is also, for the duration of the film at any rate, definitive.

9. 'Hope you enjoyed the music tonight'

As in Kubrick's earlier films, the music heard in *Eyes Wide Shut* combines a selection of existing pieces with an original score by a woman composer (Wendy Carlos for *The Shining*, Abigail Mead – pseudonym of Vivian Kubrick – for *Full Metal Jacket*). But the two most characteristic pieces were taken from Ligeti and Shostakovich.

Ligeti's piano piece, with its repeated notes like the merciless blows of a hammer, is heard no less than five times,[17] each time in a different way: when Bill appears before the secret society, when he is given a typed letter of warning outside the Somerton mansion, when he is followed through the streets of Greenwich Village, when, having taken refuge in a café, he reads the article about Amanda Curran's 'overdose' and, lastly, when he sees the mask he wore lying on the conjugal bed. In my opinion, this imperious music embodies the Law.

Shostakovich's waltz is heard less often, but at crucial points: as well as the opening and closing credits, it accompanies the montage of Bill and Alice's daily routine. In my view it represents Life.

Jocelyn Pook was given the important task of composing the music associated with the stories told by Alice (the naval officer and the erotic dream), Bill's fantasised images of Alice's sexual encounter and the Somerton orgy. For the orgy Pook created a sort of 'world music' quite similar to the erotico-religious recordings of the band Enigma, with a male voice played backwards evoking some kind of eastern priest. For the Cape Cod story she created a beautiful, mysterious piece whose oscillating tones are dominated by stringed instruments.

Listening again to these different pieces of music, it becomes apparent that they have thematic links, beyond any differences of genre and origin. For example Ligeti's *Musica ricercata*, the standard 'Strangers in the Night' (in Somerton), Chris Isaak's song entitled 'Baby Did a Bad Bad Thing' (heard when Alice and Bill kiss), the anonymous male voice heard singing backwards in the sequence of the ritual before the orgy and

Nick playing the keyboards at Somerton

the start of Jocelyn Pook's music for the walk through the various rooms in which couples are fornicating all share a melodic oscillation of two adjacent degrees (that is, which are adjacent in the scale), the interval being either a major or minor second. In concrete terms Ligeti oscillates between F and F sharp, Isaak between E and F sharp, the 'backwards' singer of the ritual between A and B, 'Migrations' in the early part of the fornication sequence between D and E flat and 'Strangers in the Night' between F and G. Was this an unintended coincidence or was it deliberately calculated? The reality is there. This observation helps to shed light on a hidden unity between most of the pieces of music that we hear in the film, whose melodies evoke something stiff, fixed or blocked in a narrow space. The melody in the piece by Shostakovich on the other hand unfolds across a much broader space of intervals.

10. 'Lou Nathanson just died'

Eyes Wide Shut was screened in New York with a provisional sound mix and incomplete post-dubbing. It seems to have been very much liked by the few who saw it, and particularly by the two actors. Kubrick apparently said that it was his best film and expressed his satisfaction with the work of his two stars. According to Jan Harlan, the relief he felt in relation to this film, which he had carried within him for so long, precipitated an internal physical change.

On 7 March 1999 the great director died suddenly in his bed, while he was sleeping, like Lou Nathanson in his film. The news quickly spread around the world and speculation grew about the now posthumous film. Sidney Pollack denied rumours that he had slightly modified the version presented to the public. It is highly likely that Kubrick would have made changes had he been able, but we must accept seeing this film as it was left after its director's death. The sound mix does of course contain a few 'holes' or moments of 'weakness', such as the sudden disappearance of the music in the ritual ceremony when Bill accompanies the mysterious woman with whom he thinks he can have sex. A fault of this kind cannot be imputed to those responsible for the film's sound, including the great English sound mixer Graham Hartstone, whose name was already linked

'Baby Did a Bad Bad Thing'

to what is for me the finest sound mix in the history of the cinema, that of *Blade Runner* (1982); rather it reflects their desire to respect the film as Kubrick left it. All the rest of the sound is perfect – extremely subtle and unobtrusive. The very many sounds of cars passing in the street, for example, are admirably spaced and paced in a way that reflects the feeling of normality, of the ebb and flow of the everyday rhythm of life. The same is true of the neighbourhood and traffic sounds that are heard in the interior scenes. Here Kubrick works with sounds like a musician who has decided to use only one instrument with six notes and three nuances, exploiting it to the maximum. This unobtrusiveness, which in no way prevents precision, enhances the quality of the actors' diction, particularly the breathy, almost whispered speech of Nicole Kidman.

There were a great many expectations surrounding this film. Because of the trailer showing the naked couple of Kidman and Cruise to the sound of 'Baby Did a Bad Bad Thing', people of course expected a film containing long, explicit sex scenes between the main characters. When the film was released in the USA on 16 July some journalists, including some from France, spread the rumour that it was a disappointment.

11. 'You have been way out of your depth'
The frequent reaction of many French newspapers on the film's release can be summed up by the question, 'What is Kubrick playing at?' What

was interesting about these characters who seemed rather pale? Why so much elegance in filming an ordinary New York couple and people who exchange such brilliant lines as 'Merry Christmas', 'Is my hair OK?', 'Michigan is a beautiful state', and so on.

Like some films by Eric Rohmer, Manoel de Oliveira or Paul Verhoeven (*Starship Troopers*, 1997) *Eyes Wide Shut* uses what could be described as cinematographic irony, in the sense that Kubrick brings great care, precision and calm to the depiction of characters and actions which we do not know whether to regard as insignificant or important, ridiculous or admirable or simply human.

Philippe Garnier, the French Los Angeles correspondent of the French daily paper *Libération*, accused the film of being senile, bourgeois and, to crown it all, implausible. In his view no Manhattan doctor living in Central Park West would ever drink Budweiser from the can, as Tom Cruise does. Others were disconcerted by the separation between the Nietzschean, transgressive, 'larger-than-life' image of Kubrick's world and the cautious morality that the film seemed to them to be advocating.

Eyes Wide Shut is also a disconcerting film because we are used – wrongly – to thinking of Kubrick as a director working to update cinematographic genres (from the war film to science fiction, via the 'period movie') and this film does not fit the pattern. It is neither a thriller (not enough crime elements), nor a comedy (Kubrick rejected witticisms and

MILICH: Doctor, sorry, what colour did you say?

only admits a discreet humour in certain scenes, such as those at the Rainbow costume-hire store), nor a tragedy (the story has a happy ending).

This does not prevent us from being reminded from time to time of David Lynch's *Blue Velvet* (1986 – a film which had previously shown a woman who has a dream and a man who falls into that dream), of Orson Welles in the grotesque nature of certain scenes (the character of Milich), and of Fellini here and there in the lunar character of several scenes or the glacial depiction of the sexual act. Yet *Eyes Wide Shut* remains a film that had never been made before and is unlike any other, including the previous films of Stanley Kubrick.

12. 'Is there something I'm missing?'

With *Eyes Wide Shut*, as with *2001: A Space Odyssey*, there is a great temptation to construct the 'perfect interpretation', which would mean that the film would no longer be any more than a coded message made transparent. The disadvantage of this approach is that it erases everything which brings a work alive and consists of details of texture and particular effects which do not necessarily have anything to do with the main theme.

The right way to work on a film – to avoid too closed an interpretation – seems to me to be to watch it several times with no precise intentions. Today's media – video tape and DVD – are aids to this kind of familiarisation; but it remains indispensable to see the film projected several times as well.

As in a police inquiry, one should not set up any hierarchies or look in any particular direction. One should not banish emotions and projections, but rather bring them to light, formulate and be aware of them, let them float.

This approach also involves abandoning any simplified overall judgment, along with everything we already know about the director through his previous films and media presence.

In this inquiry there is ultimately neither criminal nor crime. Our goal will simply be to raise a few hypotheses to cast light on the way that a film 'speaks' to us and what it 'speaks' about.

A film is a system, not of meanings, but of signifiers. We must go in search of these signifiers (the pattern of 'two adjacent notes' in the various pieces of music, the parroting effects I shall discuss later on; a shot of a man walking recalling another man walking in a rhyming effect)[18] and we can do this only by means of a non-intentional method; for in cinema, that art that fixes rhythms, substances, forms, figures and all kinds of other things onto a single support, the signifier can sit anywhere.

At the same time we must watch the film as though continually rediscovering it; we must retain the traces of our very first impressions, of all that was charming, intriguing or boring at first sight, while also never censoring what we have understood or not understood first time round.

The first time I saw *Eyes Wide Shut* I found it sublime, with two areas of frustration. The first was that Nicole Kidman is not seen at greater length; the second was that the sequence in the Somerton palace seemed to me to be atrociously boring, particularly the middle section.

After watching it again countless times, I can accept that Kidman's role is no longer: the frustration I felt was certainly not intended by Kubrick, but may stem from the exceptional success of her early scenes (the dance with the Hungarian, the 'moment of truth' in the bedroom), where she is so seductive and full of life that one could spend the entire film watching her. The greatest director in the world cannot prevent a film from becoming 'unbalanced' sometimes, not because an actor is not as good but because that actor is much better than we thought.

As for the weakness of the scenes at the Somerton palace, I still have the feeling that Kubrick had not found the right way to do them. Fellini found a solution for the orgy in his *Casanova* (1976): the characters, men and women, were not naked, but acted as though they were. Here the real nudity of the participants, in practice primarily that of the women (we never see the men's penises), slender creatures with artistically shaved pubic hair reminiscent of a photograph by Helmut Newton, does not hit the right note between realism and stylisation.

Next comes the question of interpretation. A film's exegesis always provides matter for discussion as, unlike a novel, where it is accepted that Anna Karenina is above all Anna Karenina, it is often based on the generalisation of a particular image or character. But what right have we to generalise what we see, giving it a different, more general or symbolic meaning from that which it has in the story, for example by regarding a character as emblematic of a category? In other words, can and should we regard Alice Harford, the young, white, American doctor's wife, played by Kidman, as representative of young, white, American doctors' wives, or of young, white, American women, or of young women, and so on? Theoretically we should see only particular stories; yet we know that a film often advances a view of a more general situation. There is surely something of every woman in Alice, of every man in Bill, while their marriage has something of every marriage.

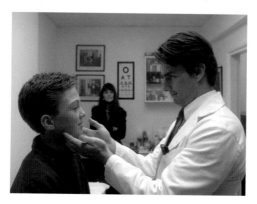

Bill in his office: 'Looking forward to Christmas?'

Cross-cutting: Alice and Helena in parallel

As an example of a scene that encourages us to 'generalise', let us look at the montage showing Bill and Alice's daily routines; two consecutive shots show each relating to a child: Alice in the Harfords' apartment brushing their little girl's hair and Bill in his office examining the jaw of a little boy who is about the same age. This presence of a little girl with Alice and a little boy with Bill may well create in us the representation of the little boy they could have had (instead of a girl) or that they could have later. But, of course, to make such a generalisation would be to disregard the facts. We have no proof, only 'clues'.

In this film interpretation becomes an issue not just for the audience, but also for the main character. Due to a number of disturbing coincidences (the meeting with Nightingale at Ziegler's, then at the Sonata Café when Nightingale is about to leave for the orgy to which he gives Bill the password; the phone call from Alice which interrupts Bill when he is about to go to bed with Domino, and above all the coincidence involving Mandy/Amanda), the film has an all-pervasive atmosphere of paranoia; everything Bill encounters can be understood by him as intentional, or calculated according to a plan, as in David Mamet's *House of Games* (1987), or David Fincher's *The Game* (1997). Every meeting, every phone call may be part of a conspiracy hatched – why not? – by Alice. After all it was she who drove Bill to stay out all night by provoking him with tales of her own sexual fantasies.

ALICE (off screen): Joe has how much more money than Mike?

The feeling of paranoia is further heightened by the precision of execution, which we sense in Kubrick's work through its sharp detail, the studied symmetry of its visual composition, clean, precise shooting and editing and finely tuned sound. If the image is so precise and deliberate, the audience thinks, it must be because the director wants to tell us something over and above the image; the words are spoken slowly and clearly because they mean something different, or something more.

But supposing there is nothing more. Supposing there are only signifiers with nothing signified.

Among other things *Eyes Wide Shut* is a film about the paranoid relationship to the world. The surprising thing is that it is also a film about everyday life.

13. 'Life goes on. It always does'

On 5 September 1970 the Russian director Andrey Tarkovsky made the following note in his *Journal*: 'Of course life has no point. If it had, man would not be free, he'd become a slave to that point and his life would be governed by completely new criteria; the criteria of slavery.'[19]

Eyes Wide Shut is a film that talks about life; a film that describes everyday life through a couple who have procreated and perpetuated life, and as such it has no precise meaning. The Shostakovich waltz, which we hear three times during the film, is expressive of movement, melancholic beauty and finitude all at once. It evokes a couple, a family – moreover, strangely, before Kubrick used it, this waltz had featured in a French television commercial for life assurance. The subject of *Eyes Wide Shut* is the everyday life of a couple of mortal human beings, from the point of view of the vastness of history and the infinity of the world.

At the start of the film, two human beings in the late 1990s talk about a Latin poet who died more than two thousand years ago. A little later Alice refers to the 'millions of years of evolution' that led to hominoids and, at the end, husband and wife talk of their future life together, he betting on 'forever', she preferring to stay within the medium close-up of a small human life, a simple portion of life itself. *Eyes Wide Shut* talks about us, western human beings living in the year 2000, looking

Life goes on in the streets of
Manhattan

back over two thousand years and seeing another thousand stretching
before us, way beyond the possible duration of our own lifetimes.

It may seem strange to link this film to everyday life, since *Eyes Wide
Shut* seems to take as its heroes two of life's privileged people, living in a
lovely apartment in New York, with no obvious material concerns (Bill is
prodigal with his hundred dollar bills) and even fewer health problems.

Yet, almost certainly, along with the erasure of any too precise cultural
identity, this is the means Kubrick found to render the story more universal.
For when one has 'everything', problems can spring only from within, from
the human psychological machine; they appear more clearly as endogenous.

Bill arrives at his office in the
morning

So, in the early part of the film everything is done to ensure that a western audience will recognise elements of their own daily lives in what happens on screen; at least this applies to a European or American audience who are not too impoverished. We see a man who is about to go out with his wife and cannot find his wallet ('Honey, have you seen my wallet?' is the first line in the film), a little girl who asks her parents if she can stay up late to watch television, and her parents who find they don't know anyone at a party where all the other guests are much richer than they are.[20] This is an important detail, for human beings experience almost everything that happens to them by comparing themselves to those whom they believe, rightly or wrongly, to be more fortunate, lucky, gifted (and so on).[21]

Furthermore, during this evening at the millionaire Ziegler's, the only acquaintance to whom the young doctor can give a friendly slap on the back is Nick Nightingale, a musician from the dance band. Bill goes only once to the home of someone poorer than himself; this is Domino's apartment, where he seems moreover to feel very comfortable. Without exception all the other private homes which he enters are places where he cannot fail to feel alone and socially inferior, places where he's told 'You don't belong here'. What human being, however rich, has not had the same feeling at one time or another?

As in life (and unlike in films where no one ever sleeps) *Eyes Wide Shut* gives us the day's work, with all its repetitive aspects (Bill's consultations, Alice's maternal tasks), the evening tiredness that sets Alice yawning, Christmas presents to be wrapped, 'Thank you' notes to be sent to the hosts of the night before, a wife eating chocolate biscuits as she waits for her husband, debts and meetings with strangers.

As in life, the married man and woman meet with extramarital temptation and, as in life, those to which they give way are far less numerous or important than those to which they do not. Everyday life is made up of the hundreds of things that we dream of doing (acting like a hero, punching someone who has been violent or rude in the street) but which remain no more than potentialities until life tells us, 'it's too late'. As in life, Bill and Alice are neither heroes nor scumbags nor adventurers; they will probably go on living together, just as in life.

Everyday life also includes basking in the euphoria provoked by drink, marijuana or flattering words from a stranger at a party, and then we have to go home and go to work the next day, 'do our face', get our child to do her homework and take her to the shops.

In the sense that *Eyes Wide Shut* is a film about 'everyday life', the shots in the street when Bill is not there are very important. Sometimes these shots of streets modestly resemble the shots used in sitcoms to establish the location (such as the two shots of the outside of the block in Central Park West where the Harfords live). These do much more than simply tell us 'we are outside Bill's home' or 'Bill is walking in midtown'. Like the city shots beloved of Ozu, they relocate everything that is happening in the continual flow of life.

Also as in real life, the heroes meet up with people they know, or have known in the past, and in whom they can see their own worst fears reflected. There is the pianist Nightingale, formerly a fellow student of Bill's at medical school, whom he meets ten years later and whose slightly cynical air and slightly bitter humour clearly give us to understand that his life has not turned out as he dreamed. Yet, in comparing himself to Nick (who, in his eyes, is taking part in a 'big adventure' by playing piano for these great orgies) Bill might wonder if it is not he himself, the dutiful doctor, who has missed out on 'real living'.

Conversely others seem to have prematurely taken a path which will be more of a repetition than an adventure: Marion will only leave her dead father's bedside to marry a maths teacher – and there again Bill (and many of us with him) might wonder, like her, have I set out too young on a well-trodden path?

Then there is Alice, with her dreams of leaving everything for a naval officer whom she did not in fact follow, passively waiting instead for him to declare his love. This is the same Alice who, at the end of the film, goes Christmas shopping with her husband and child.

It is all just like life, with the single difference that the other usual obstacles (money problems, the problem of being ugly, ordinary or good-looking, healthy or sick, issues of exclusion linked to skin colour or ethnic origins) have been deliberately removed by the director in the case of our two protagonists. All that remains is naked human nature.

As is often the case, Kubrick is interested in what does not go right when everything should be working fine, when the computer is well-designed (*2001: A Space Odyssey*), the regiment of marines well-trained (*Full Metal Jacket*), the logic of nuclear deterrence perfect (*Dr Strangelove*, 1963), when a man has adopted all available means to overcome his humble origins and climb to the top of the social ladder (*Barry Lyndon*) or to write the book of his dreams (*The Shining*) and here when the protagonists are young, attractive, wealthy, healthy and open-minded …

They are all this, but they are neither heroes nor anti-heroes. They are moreover without any illusions on this point. When the two models try to seduce Bill and one of them reminds him of the gentlemanly way that he lent her a handkerchief, he says, self-mockingly, 'That's the kind of hero I can be sometimes.' In the last scene of the film, Alice speaks with gentle irony of their respective 'adventures', in which neither of them has behaved magnificently.

This makes them an intimate, loving and close couple. But the film has to separate them to bring them back together. At the beginning we think we're going to follow them both; a little later on we are surprised by the change of tack.

14. 'You have to go out again, tonight?'

A Clockwork Orange starts in a lyrical, baroque style, its sets describing a world of anticipation in an uncertain, nocturnal future; then, from the moment that Alex is imprisoned, it depicts an increasingly diurnal world, ever more closely resembling contemporary England. *Full Metal Jacket* begins by concentrating on the training of the marines, and among other things on the relationship between the sergeant and Private Pyle, both of whom die forty minutes into the film – and suddenly we are in Vietnam and they are no longer mentioned. *2001* makes enormous leaps in time, changing characters along the way.

However what is new in *Eyes Wide Shut* compared to Kubrick's earlier films is that he does it all discreetly and without warning. The film

Alice no. 2, before
telephoning her husband

begins with cross-cutting between Bill and Alice (shown now together,
now separately); Kubrick then drops the cross-cutting to concentrate
mainly on Bill. With the exception of the imaginary Alice seen mentally by
Bill in black-and-white, the real Alice is no longer present when Bill is not
looking at her, except in two very short – and therefore all the more
significant – shots: when she is in the kitchen smoking a cigarette and
eating chocolate biscuits, then rings Bill, and when when she is seen
sleeping next to the mask, before Bill finds her.

Cross-cutting always has a double meaning, since it suggests
associations that are both spatio-temporal (while Bill is preparing to be
unfaithful to his wife, Alice stays at home) and logical and formal, suggesting
a contrast (while he is unfaithful and stays out all night, she stays in the
marital home) or, on the contrary, a similarity (Alice and Bill are each seen
deep in the routine of their respective everyday occupations).

15. 'The blindfold wasn't on so well'

The film also contains two Alices, the one elusive, the other on screen far
more often. Both have something in common: we never see them in the
street; they exist only in the artificial light of a bathroom, a ballroom and a
party, never once outside. It is in dreams and in speech that these two
Alices walk through space. Even in Bill's fantasies Alice is enclosed in a
room.

The first Alice is naked, turned into a statue and magnified, as we see her at the very beginning, taking off her dress for the audience's eyes alone. This shot creates the first image of Alice and at once fulfils the desire of the audience to see Nicole Kidman naked; as a result the rest of the story is, as it were, relieved of this expectation and, at the same time, one of the classic sources of suspense is broken (as if the murderer's identity were shown at the start). This initial shot of Alice is framed twice: in space by two columns and in time by the two titles of the credits, one showing the director's name and the other the title, which, being placed immediately after the image we have just seen, is thereby associated with sex and voyeurism.

This isolated shot of Alice no. 1 undressing is also reminiscent of the silent cinema in which, very often and particularly in introductory scenes, a character is seen in images which are not tied to any particular point in the action, framed by two intertitles. Here we may choose to locate the image of Alice before the evening at Ziegler's (Alice trying on her dresses) but we can also see it as a thing in itself, as a portrait.

The other image of Alice no. 1, which exists only for the audience, figures in the 'montage' of the Harfords' daily lives, when her naked body is seen from a low angle as she is putting on a black bra, as though putting on her battle armour. However each time she is shown in this way, with her body magnified, Kubrick shows her just afterwards as Alice no. 2, in other words as a real, particular woman in the bathroom. The first time is the

Alice no. 1, doubly framed, at the beginning of the film

initial scene mentioned at the beginning of this book. Similarly Alice no. 1 putting on her bra is soon followed by Alice no. 2 in her underclothes with her daughter (two women, one learning her femininity) putting deodorant on her armpits and sniffing herself.

So the film begins with Alice no. 1 and ends with Alice no. 2, the one who wears glasses and talks to her husband in a shop. Woman with a capital 'W' has been replaced by a woman.

A bridge between the image-Alice and the individual woman-Alice is made in the shot in which she takes off her earrings in front of a mirror and her husband comes in and starts to kiss her. Here Alice is at once an image and a wife to her husband.

We should note that, having opened with a voyeuristic approach, the film then becomes very vague on the theme of voyeurism, a theme so often invoked by cinema since its beginnings. The history of cinema is full of shots taken through a hole in the wall, of nakedness seen through a half-open door, the steamed-up glass of a shower, a blind, in a reflection, not to mention telescopes (*Body Double*, 1984) and cameras (*Rear Window*, 1954). While the film's first shot is one for the voyeurs, allowing us alone to glimpse Nicole Kidman between two columns, this theme returns in almost no other single shot in the entire film. For example it is not clear whether Bill goes to the Somerton orgy as a peeping Tom or to make love. And what are all the watching couples, including those who are naked, doing? What are they watching?

16. 'Just a glance. Nothing more'

In Fellini's *8½* (1962), everything is played out through the dark glasses worn by Guido Anselmi, the director's shifty alter-ego played by Marcello Mastroianni. When Guido takes these glasses off or looks over the top of them, another world appears, more satisfying than the real one, in which he is the lord of a harem full of obliging women. They become the open door to this world. However while he has them on he remains locked away in his guilt and indecision.

Kubrick chose to have Alice wear clear glasses and, from time to time, she takes them off, or does not wear them. These glasses, which we

Alice is at once an image and a wife to her husband

see her wearing at the beginning and which she then takes off before going out for the evening with Bill, draw our attention to what she sees, or sees in what she is saying. She is not wearing them when she tells the story of the man in Cape Cod or recounts her dreams; she has them on her nose in the final dialogue with Bill.

In the short scene on which the trailer was based, in which she is in front of the mirror, she is wearing these glasses and takes them off when Bill caresses her and she responds to his kisses. What does she see then, when she turns her eyes to the mirror?

What does she see in another family scene in which, while helping her daughter do her arithmetic, she looks over her glasses at her husband Bill in the kitchen (who at that moment is recalling her account of her dream in which she said, 'I was fucking other men')?

Here we see a look, but we do not know what that look sees in turn.

17. 'I'm gonna go to bed now'

At the beginning of the film Alice goes out in the evening. At the end she goes out during the day – for the first time.

Every film, any film, is a series of first times: the first time characters are called by name; the first time their professional and family identity is given, the first time they meet another character, that they sleep, and so

Wife, husband and child in
the toy shop

on. 'First times' are spaced according to the needs of the script, but also
help to give the film its shape and sometimes mark out its trajectory.

Thus the final scene is the first in which wife, husband and child are
all together in a place that is not their home but a toy shop, full of sales
staff and customers. In this alone, this scene introduces a new element.
Even though, in this scene, the Harfords speak only to each other, we see
them surrounded by normal life, one family among many, 'hopefully for a
long time to come'.

In practice, until this point Alice has seldom left her house. Her
reclusiveness emphasises the fact that at the same time she travels in her
imagination; for, awake or sleeping, she has dreams (the fantasy she
relates) that open up a much larger area than the parallel space through
which her husband moves. She dreams of the cosmos, of travel ... At any
rate, this creates a feeling that, when Bill escapes from home, he
rediscovers the mental space into which his wife escapes without going
out. This is the eternal story of Ulysses who, still far from home before his
return to Penelope and the marital house, is 'taken in hand' by a series of
more or less protective, tempting or maternal women (Calypso, Nausicaa,
and the goddess Athene), who are all echoes of his wife.

So Alice does not leave home, but she does dream. The man does not
dream (he never recounts his dreams), but he does go out. He walks, he goes
into the street, where he is presented with different realities and a series of tests.

18. 'Sorry, Dr Harford. Sorry to interrupt'

Bill is, as I have said, not a very rewarding character; the audience is tempted to criticise him. Yet he is like us, because he often seems inactive or guided by circumstance.

Bill is prevented on five occasions from doing what he is about to do: when he is going to 'where the rainbow ends' with the two models (but one of the Zieglers' servants comes looking for him); when he might be going to tell Alice how he feels after the Cape Cod story (but the phone rings); after Marion's declaration of love, which might have unsettled him (but Carl rings the doorbell); when he is going to go to bed with Domino (but his wife phones him); and when he might be going to overcome the resistance of the mysterious woman by force (but a masked servant comes looking for him). Each time we will never know whether he would have held himself back of his own accord from these various 'temptations'. He has no means of testing his will, since the opportunity to do something on his own initiative is always taken away from him. This adventure in which his life has possibly been saved is at the same time an adventure in which he has not been able to test his courage in any way. In one sense it has taken everything away from him.

On another occasion Bill does not react, but we do not know whether his lack of reaction is due to cowardice, indifference or a position of weakness. This is when he is insulted by a group of youths and one of

GAYLE: Well, let's find out

them hits him. However his lack of reaction is not emphasised by the editing, or by any close-up of his face in which we could 'read' his feelings.

On the other hand we see him begin two movements which he does not finish, stopping himself for some inner reason which remains unknown to us: we see him bend over the dead Amanda Curran (to kiss her? to read the secret hidden in her half-closed, dead woman's eyes?), then straighten up and step back, in a silent pause between two pieces of music by Liszt, there being no external factor to tear him away from this in explicable impulse.[22] The other time is the half-begun move to kiss Domino's hand at the end of their scene together.

In this strange story's narrative we share, or think we share, the 'point of view' of a character who ultimately remains secretive.

19. 'I know what happened last night'

Like Schnitzler's story, with the exception of one important scene, Kubrick's film is told from Bill's point of view: we do not enter into Alice's thoughts and, two or three domestic shots aside, we do not know what she does when Bill is not there, beyond what she tells him.

But the question of 'point of view' is not the same in a written story as it is in cinema. In the cinema the 'point of view' is only suggested. It is linked, in particular, to the question of 'in whose presence' the scene takes place. If a character is in almost all the scenes – as Bill is – with two or three 'exceptions', the film will be regarded as being told from his point of view, although we see him just as we see the other characters, from the outside. Another important question is that of knowledge: do we know less than the character, or more, or as much? Do we share his 'secrets'? In the case of Bill we do, since we alone follow him through different situations whose connections are in principle known only to him (and us).

In a certain number of shots, particularly those of the montage of everyday life, we see Alice separate from her husband, unseen by him; however this is always in a state (nakedness) or doing things (her housewifely tasks) which are very familiar to him, perhaps too familiar, and in which he can easily imagine her. So in principle these shots do not disrupt Bill's point of view.

With the exception of one important scene. This is of course the scene in which Alice and the suave Hungarian dance together, fragmented by cross-cutting. Although Bill can see what they are doing from a distance, he will never know what Alice said, nor will he be aware of her exemplary wifely conduct. In the scene where husband and wife are back in their bedroom together, in their underclothes, we are witness to the fact that, instead of telling Bill what we saw (she asserted her status as a happily married woman and chose to evade her admirer's advances), she prefers to give her husband, who is too 'sure of himself', something to be jealous about. We are also in a position to compare Alice's behaviour with Sandor and the way she tells Bill her 'fantasies'. She has not been unfaithful to him in reality, but she wants to convince him that she has been unfaithful in her thoughts.

The cinema audience is in an ambiguous position: they know both more and less than each of the characters in isolation, but this knowledge is all logical speculation, which they know the film can overturn like a set of skittles from one moment to the next. Through cross-cutting they know that Alice does not have a lover she sees while her husband is at work; but the ellipses in this cross-cutting enable them to imagine that there are things they have not been shown, and which they will not discover until the end.

The question is not what we know, but the form in which we learn it.

20. 'I'll tell you everything'
There are two big ellipses in the story of *Eyes Wide Shut*:

- When, after caressing each other naked in front of the mirror, Bill and Alice make love (if that is what they do). This ellipsis is interesting, as it gives Alice's final word 'fuck' its full potency. We do not know whether they have been sexually indifferent to each other, although everything would suggest that Alice is not motivated by any lukewarm attitude to sex on the part of her husband. However the fact that we do not see them making love, although they probably do, gains its full meaning from the fact that we do see the black-and-white scenes of Alice's imaginary love-making on several occasions. Strangely, this short scene in which husband and wife caress each other while looking in the mirror takes on a perverse quality – with the aid of the word 'bad' in Chris Isaak's song – and introduces a third party – or two third parties – represented by their reflections.

• When Bill tells Alice everything, after finding the mask in his place in the marital bed. There is nothing to indicate how much of what we have seen he has told Alice, and above all how he has told it, whether he has talked about his feelings – for her as well as for the various women he has met – and so on. No matter that this may be motivated by a fear of boring us with the story of events that we have witnessed. It would undoubtedly be a different film (and a different short story) were we to hear the language Bill uses to recount what has happened and the details he includes. We should have the surprise and irritation of an indelible comparison between what we have seen 'from the outside' and the character's verbalisation of it. The fact that we do not hear Bill's story allows all that has happened and that we have witnessed to take on the meaning of an implicit story told to Alice, making her the retrospective witness of all that we have seen.

A third, more subtle yet no less important ellipsis, is contained in the same gap of time, before we see the couple in the morning, when Alice's nose is red from crying. It covers the story of the mask: how she found it, what she thought and what she felt. This ellipsis suddenly separates us from the characters: they return to their secrets and their intimacy; we shall soon be ready to leave them.

Other, no less important ellipses occur in the scene with Ziegler. These are ellipses of behaviour and speech.

21. 'I have to be completely frank'
The 'revelation' scene with Ziegler in the billiard room cannot be summed up as: 'Ziegler tells Bill that the woman's sacrifice was staged.' In what order does Ziegler tell Bill this? At what time? After stating what else? Lastly, what 'gap' do his explanations fail to fill? This is what matters.

This scene is striking for the theatrical and always ambiguous nature of Victor Ziegler's attitude: he speaks nervously, says two or three times that he is going to tell the real truth, 'tempts' Bill ('If I were to tell you who those people were … but I'm not going to tell you'), is friendly, gets angry, is tense, plays with everything he touches, hesitates, sits in a chair and on the billiard table, gets up, walks about, sits down again, pours Bill a whisky and so on, in such a way that we are continually wondering whether he is acting all the time or only now and then, and above all why he is acting.

If we look carefully, from time to time we see that the actor seems to be 'acting badly' in terms of the classical criteria of cinema, since he seems to know in advance what he is going to say and do, while pretending to be

In Ziegler's bathroom, Mandy vanishes

ZIEGLER: Alice … you're absolutely stunning

spontaneous. When he says his lines they sound as though they were already formed in his head.

The entire billiard room scene is a puzzle which seems to fall apart as it is being completed. It is built around an at least partial 'explanation' of the various mysteries: Who had Bill followed (Ziegler)? Who was the woman who 'gave' herself to Bill (a prostitute)? What did she die of (an overdose)? What happened to Nightingale (he was put on a plane out of the city)? However the entire puzzle is pulled to pieces by Ziegler's constant changes of attitude – from friendliness to anger, nervousness to assurance, seriousness to vulgarity. Nor do we understand why he holds back information that he could have provided at the beginning of the scene, only giving it at the very end, which makes it seem unreliable. He states that everything Bill saw at the 'orgy' was 'staged' while he himself is acting as though his role has been written in advance, or like a man who has lied, then decided to stop lying, and has got lost in the labyrinth of his own lies.

Ziegler does not use concrete terms. He says, 'I was there, I saw everything', but he does not say, 'I am the man who made you a sign from the top of the stairs, the man who sent you a woman' and Bill does not ask him. For if he was not the man in the three-cornered hat, who was he? And if it was him, why did he send Bill a woman?[23]

Yet Ziegler is like a father; he is all the more clearly seen in a father's image because Bill is of an age to be his son and we know nothing about Victor's children (if he has any), or what has happened to Bill's parents (who are never mentioned). Ziegler's sudden vulgar outbursts create an atmosphere of manly complicity (this is a 'men only' scene).

When Ziegler makes his characteristic noisy pout after describing Amanda Curran's death from an overdose (this woman whose name he never utters – another 'gap'), it is very shocking because he is talking about a human being and, what's more, a woman he has slept with. The noise he makes also conveys the fact that death is an unthinkable point between before and after. After this he becomes friendly and paternal towards Bill.

This makes us forget that Bill is himself a father. There are two 'real' fathers in the film, Milich and Bill. While the former is 'dodgy' from various points of view (he prostitutes his daughter), it is hard for us to see the latter as the father that he nevertheless is.

His daughter calls him 'Daddy', greets him with joy, is proud to show him her marks and often looks at him (toy shop scene). Yet he remains distant. It is as though, in his eyes, mother and daughter together form a separate female group and everything goes through Alice or in her presence. While Alice never prevents Bill from having contact with his daughter – on the contrary, she refers to him as 'Daddy' in his absence – it is he who tends to distance himself. He never talks about his daughter when she is not there and never mentions her by name.

The only scene in which he is alone with Helena is when, returning from his wild night, he briefly and silently looks in on her as she sleeps in her toy-filled room. The absence of any words is very moving.

22. 'You're gonna have to wait and see'

In *2001* Heywood Floyd's little girl, who seems to be an only child, is contacted by her father from a space station. For her birthday she asks him for a bushbaby; later in the film this request is forgotten. We see all kinds of marvellous things, but we never find out if the little girl's hopeful wish has been fulfilled.[24]

More than thirty years later the promise seems about to be kept, because here is another little girl, seemingly of the same age, who has been

Heywood Floyd and his daughter in *2001: A Space Odyssey*

let loose in a toy shop. Here she sees various things she would like for Christmas: she wants a puppy, but is then attracted by a pram for her doll Sabrina, then by a giant teddy bear like the one she already has. In short the film leaves unanswered the question of what Christmas present the little girl will eventually choose.

Her parents encourage her to go off so that they can exchange some serious moments of truth. Once again, we will not find out whether she has received the object of her desire. This leaves us free to imagine that the 'present' will be a little brother, that her parents will have another child, born of their rediscovered union.

23. 'Looking forward to Christmas?'

Schnitzler's story symbolically unfolded at the end of winter, a time when the forces of spring and rebirth are awakening. Kubrick and Raphael skilfully transposed the action to just before Christmas. This setting is made clear from the beginning by the Harfords' Christmas tree and is frequently re-emphasised throughout the film by both situations and dialogue (the Zieglers receiving their guests, Helena and her mother wrapping up a large book for 'Daddy', the Harfords talking about presents still to be wrapped), even the dialogue in a cartoon that Helena watches in the kitchen, or when Bill says to a little boy he is examining, 'Looking forward to Christmas?' It also provides a reason to fill the images with active light sources, through the systematic appearance of Christmas trees, fairy lights and Christmas wreaths in every set, with the exception of one. So the coming of Christmas is visible everywhere, lighting the image from within and making it radiate light.

At the same time this context enables the film to reveal a society that has 'forgotten' or abandoned the meaning of the religious festivals that occur at regular intervals in its calendar. Christmas has become simply an opportunity to host magnificent parties and give presents to children. Neither the name of Jesus nor his image, nor any crosses or cradles are ever shown or mentioned, even as an oath.[25] Even in the room of the man who has just died – and whose name suggests he is Jewish – no religious rites occur or are alluded to. Similarly no one mentions the hypothesis of an afterlife or the survival of the soul. Death seems absolute and definitive.

In Bill's office

Bill arrives in a taxi outside at
the Rainbow boutique

Christmas is a birthday; it celebrates the anniversary of a little boy's
birth, from whose date a large proportion of our world counts time. In
2001 birthdays play an important role for human beings. Even Hal the
computer can rattle off his 'date of birth'.

However there is one place, only one in the entire film, where there
are no signs of Christmas and where, at the same time, characters dress up
like members of a sect, to carry out a sacred sexual ritual: this is the
Somerton mansion. Here we seem to be outside time, if not outside space,
where anonymous and collective coitus, from which any notion of pleasure
is strangely absent, seems to be creating new lives.

24. 'Something we need to do as soon as possible'

Eyes Wide Shut is not set in any particular year; however the presence and shape of the mobile phones tell us that we are in the late 1990s of the twentieth century. The approach of a symbolic event as important as was the date of 31 December 1999, on a scale much larger than the life of an individual, widens the contrasts between the here and now and the future, creating both urgency and a feeling of infinite time: this event, which was such a long time coming, would be gone in a few seconds.

For those who like it, *Eyes Wide Shut* is a 'magical' film that transports us beyond time. For example, Alice and Sandor's dance seems to go on and on forever because it is split into five parts, cross-cut with what is happening to Bill at the same time. However the rhythm of the dialogue and scenes also makes an important contribution to this feeling.

The characters in *Eyes Wide Shut* seem to have all the time they need. They are seldom interrupted, seldom in a hurry (other than because of the cold when they are walking in the street) and, apart from the beginning ('We are late'), are never late. They say 'Hello' and 'Thank you' and take the time to answer questions, often repeating them before they answer ('parroting', which we shall discuss later). Sometimes they even pause for a moment between each word, or wait several seconds before picking up the phone (Bill Harford when he is told that Nathanson has died). The waitress at Gillespie's has no other clients to serve at the same time as Bill; the conversation between Bill and the desk clerk is not interrupted by any hotel clients returning their keys. No one runs in this film; cars pass at moderate speed, no fingers stab at a lift button, no one charges down a staircase four steps at a time.

According to Raphael, as we have said, from the writing stage onwards Kubrick emphasised the need to respect a particular tempo. It is this that gives so much weight to one of the last lines in the film, when Alice says that there is something she and her husband must do 'as soon as possible'. Suddenly, something has become urgent. It is as though a film is sometimes a long preparation and, suddenly, something must be radically changed.

The paradox of a film in which the characters sometimes have loads of time and sometimes everything happens very fast – too fast – is the image of time in cinema, which is made of dilations and precipitations, stable yet unbalanced states and sudden, radical shifts.

Marion talks to Dr Harford about her father's death, in the presence of her father's corpse, and suddenly, when he is leaning towards her, she gives way to something, changes completely. We realise that everything that had happened until then was hanging on that moment.

The fact that cinema time is not regular or linear is due, among other things of course, to the principle of editing, which punctuates what is said or will be said, done or will be done in an irregular way, with no pre-established rhythm. However it is also due (and this remark may seem odd) to the fact that cinema dialogue is usually spoken and in prose, with no predictable cadence.

BILL: It really could be a wonderful change for you, Marion

Marion before her sudden decision

In the cinema what is called slowness – the concrete awareness of
time passing, characteristic of the 'chronographic' art of sound cinema[26] –
has a fatal meeting with its opposite, its inverted image, in the 'cut', which
resembles a sudden decision. This can be said of the cut which ends the
last scene of the film on the image of Alice, who has just uttered the word
'fuck', followed by the final credits, at which point everything is tied up.[27]
The film is now closed. It is contained within two borders of time and
everything that happens within those borders, between the two cuts of the
beginning and the end, now takes on a definitive meaning and can be
interpreted, like all that happens in the time of a psychoanalytic session.

So why should the person writing this book not see a meaning for
the entire film being decided in a few seconds, in which Carl walks the
same distance that Bill has just walked?

25. 'I was actually on my way out'

Bill is in a taxi. He is going to the home of a man called Nathanson. The
images of his wife stripping naked for another man, in a hotel room, are
beginning to haunt him.

Shot of an empty hallway in a luxury apartment block. Bill enters
from the left and walks to the right, with the camera panning to follow
him. We hear a doorbell. Cut. We are inside and a woman in a maid's
uniform enters from the right and opens the door, having looked through
the spy-hole. There is a brief conversation. She does not show the way to
the dead man's room, to which Bill walks with an even tread. The camera
follows him from behind. There is a corner, Bill turns right, the camera
continues to follow him from behind, and then Bill turns left to a door on
which he gently knocks. 'Come in' calls a woman's off-screen voice,
distorted by sorrow.

Cut to a darkened room. Bill enters from the right, there is a small
Christmas tree on a cupboard. Marion is seen from the front, Bill from
behind. We do not see the dead man straight away.

The camera pans left. We see the dead man in a wide shot, lying in a
double bed. He is a little fat, aged about sixty. Bill goes to the head of the
bed and touches the dead man's forehead, without speaking. Without a

cut the camera pans left to right on Bill, who moves away from the bed. The dead man has been seen only quickly, as the camera moves, but remains present in our minds throughout the following scene, since he is now off-screen during the dialogue between Bill and Marion, 'reappearing' only with Carl's entrance, again in a shot that follows the latter's movement.

Let us go back to the point where Bill, still in the same shot in which he touched the dead man, sits in an armchair next to Marion. They are separated by a table with a lighted lamp.

Sometimes one of the faces is tightly framed, leading us to forget the presence of the material obstacle, as though there were direct

The camera follows Bill, who heads for the dead man's room

Carl, a few minutes later

communication between the two characters, or between us and the character in shot (this ambiguity is important). Sometimes a wider framing includes the separating element in the shot, with the faces of one or both characters, thereby reminding us of the presence of the obstacle.

As at other points, when one of the characters is isolated in close-up (Marion in this case), the person in the reverse shot is always framed more widely. This allows us to sense the presence of the other person and, in some cases, to see the obstacle. The sequence is dominated by shots of Marion. Perfect symmetry and a balance between shots and reverse shots is not attained until the final scene in which, when we see either husband or wife, the other retains some slight presence in the image (although Bill is in almost all the scenes, Kubrick rarely fails to point out, through camera angles and framing, that the women he is with are taller than he is,[28] so that they often look down on Bill with a kind of tenderness, as though on a child.)

At one point Bill, seen in profile, leans towards Marion (his head is lower) – and for the first time his face in close-up enters the same shot as hers, with no obstacle between them. It is then that Marion cracks and suddenly kisses Bill, as though she had fallen into a hole, or through an opening.

We sense that the situation could develop, but the doorbell we have heard once before when Bill arrived – a bell as old and traditional as the rest of the surroundings – is heard again.

Cut. We are in the hall. This time Rosa is already at the door, but she is seen from the right, from the opposite direction from which she was seen when Bill arrived. Carl, the maths teacher whom Marion has just mentioned, comes into the apartment – he is a young man with glasses and dark hair and is about as tall as Bill. He is seen from the front (unlike Bill earlier). He walks the same distance at a sure, regular pace, just as Bill did, and turns right; but the camera pivots so that, when he approaches the bedroom door, he is seen from behind, just as Bill was earlier. When he taps at the door Marion's voice once again says 'Come in'. Cut. We are once again in the bedroom. Carl enters from left to right (the camera films him from the opposite angle to that from which it filmed Bill earlier) and walks towards Marion with his hands open, like someone who has mentally rehearsed his gesture. It is in following Carl as he walks towards Marion that we once again see the image of the dead man in the background, the dead man whom we have not seen since the beginning of the scene, when Bill touched him. The dead man – whom none of the three characters present looks at – is present in the shot that brings them together, separating Marion and Carl on the one hand from Bill on the other.

But when Bill goes out with Carl ('I'll show you out'), we are left with a close-up of Marion's face, apparently in distress. In this way, at the end of three different scenes, the film is punctuated by the three faces of people whom Bill has, as it were, abandoned, and who could have had or dreamed of having an affair with him: Marion, the gay desk clerk, and Domino's roommate Sally.

The shot of Carl's entrance, which we have described in detail, as he walks towards the dead man's bedroom door, is the first in the film to show the complete action of a character who is alone and is neither Bill nor Alice. This character repeats almost exactly what Bill has done a few minutes earlier – even though it is not from the same angle – thereby creating an effect of *déjà vu*. The two men are like two billiard balls: Carl covers the same distance as Bill did before him, knocks at the door just as he did, hears the 'same' 'Come in' and enters as Bill did (with a more

BILL: Marion, your father was very proud of you

theatrical, prepared attitude) and, as in a billiard game, knocks Bill out of his place. His presence signifies that Bill can stay no longer, that there is one person too many.

Kubrick's very particular way of using a tracking shot with a wide angle lens to follow someone walking down a corridor, through a maze or a narrow passageway, and giving the character's progress an epic, fatal, conquering or irresistible air – which first came to general attention in *Paths of Glory* – often seems to mean: there is no living space for two men. I appropriate the space I cross: I clear the space before me …

When, later, Bill makes a phone call from his office, where he has stayed on alone, there is a cut to the entrance of the Nathansons' apartment, easily recognised from its décor and darkness. This is the first and last time in the film that we go to a place which does not contain either Bill or Alice. Once again Carl walks posedly into shot and picks up a phone on a table. At the other end no one speaks. Someone has definitively taken the place that Bill might have thought he could save for himself.

These two shots of Carl, exceptions in the film's narrative system, are striking for a similarity between Bill and Carl which is hard to pin down: they are like, if not identical twins, at least two brothers. When Carl picks up the phone and, at the other end, Bill decides not to speak, their black hair falls in a similar lock.

Among the many spreading echoes of the interminable shooting of *Eyes Wide Shut*, we have read that Kubrick took several dozen different takes of what is apparently a simple 'transition' shot in which Bill goes and taps on Marion's door. In contradiction of my rule of never allowing anecdotes about the making of a film to influence the analysis of that film, this made me pay attention to the shot from the first time I saw it. It awoke in me the memory of another shot in *A Clockwork Orange*, in which a boy in glasses, who is living at the writer's home, opens the door to Alex as if, bizarrely, he were the son adopted by the writer in Alex's place. There is the same feeling of someone who has taken possession of the house, and whose presence definitively excludes the hero.

In *Eyes Wide Shut* I chose to interpret this as meaning that it is Bill's own future son, in a future where Bill can never meet him, that Bill has

The bespectacled boy in *A Clockwork Orange*

just seen in Carl. Either he will suddenly have grown older, or he will be dead, or the son will have taken his place in his wife's heart. We should recall, in *2001*, the shots of the last scene in which Dave Bowman meets another, older man, resembling a rival who is himself in the future and is not him.[29]

The eviction of Bill by Carl Thomas is also like that of Barry Lyndon by Lord Bullingdon.

Bill is ripe for death, ready to accept his own mortality, in the person of another man who will be born into the family. Bill may still live to a ripe old age, but he no longer feels immortal.

The mask on Bill's bed, in his place, separated from his face, is himself, is this son. He and his wife do not talk about this mask and will not, it seems,

The mask on Bill's bed, in his place

ever talk about it. Bill weeps, his wife pulls him to her breast like a child, Bill's face is up against the mask that is a different reflection of himself.

He doesn't talk about it, as he didn't talk about the body of Lou Nathanson before him in the present, or that of Amanda Curran.

26. 'How do you spell Nuala?'

A little girl reads a simple phrase, laboriously focusing on each word ('jump … into … my … bed'); a young model sensuously spells the letters of her first name: N-U-A-L-A; a hospital receptionist carefully spells the name of a dead patient: C-U-R-R-A-N – each time the formation of the words, of the parts, the letters of the name is stripped bare.

NUALA: N-U-A-L-A

CLERK: Well, umm … *Bill*

In *Eyes Wide Shut* people take their time, not only in answering but also in speaking. It is a film unique in its speech rhythms. An emblematic scene in this respect is the one where, under the influence of marijuana, Alice starts asking Bill about the two girls: 'Tell … me … something … those … two girls …' and so on. It is almost the opposite of the films of Orson Welles, and of course of some films by Howard Hawks, in which speeches are frequently interrupted.

In *Eyes Wide Shut* forming words is an active choice – it is not always an easy, natural thing: each word seems to be acted or studied. Behind the words that are spoken we imagine all those that could have been said in their place. Like a chess move which takes the place of ten possible moves.

27. 'I don't quite know how to say this'

Most of the decisive scenes in *Eyes Wide Shut* rely entirely on what the characters say and deal with things for which we have no material or physical proof other than their words: Alice's speech in which she recounts her memories and dreams; Ziegler's speech describing what really happened at the orgy; Sally's speech telling Bill about Domino's state of health. There is nothing, not a photograph, manuscript, document, video or photocopy, to support what is said.

We see no trace of contusion on the face of Nightingale (the one that flew away); we do not see the report from Domino's blood test, nor any concrete memory of the naval officer. A spoken word can be taken back at any time (Milich), while Amanda Curran's body in the morgue bears no traces. All bodies are smooth, we are shown no physical details that might reveal the traces of what has happened to a person on their face.

When Sally says that Domino is ill, when Ziegler says that Amanda Curran was a prostitute, will Bill turn investigator and hunt down traces, evidence? Not at all. *Eyes Wide Shut* is a film in which there is a maximum of speech and a minimum of tangible proof.

Everything comes down to speech: true or false, what is said counts. The question of sincerity or fabulation is not posed.

It makes no difference whether Alice invented the memory of the naval officer – whom Bill does not apparently remember – or whether he

ALICE: I was ready to give up everything

really existed. In some cases we have nothing but speech; above and beyond truth or falsehood, speech acts; it exists.

Ultimately it is solely through speech ('Can you open your eyes, Mandy') and not by using some injection or medication that Bill 'resuscitates' the naked young woman suffering from a drug overdose at Ziegler's. *Eyes Wide Shut* consists of people confronted with speech.

Never complicit with speech, showing no evidence either for or against what is said, nor faces that 'betray' it, the images become differently invested by the audience: they become the absolute mask, which does not reproduce expressive features and movements on the outside, far less the inner being of the characters. The images become what does not reveal.

28. 'It's a password. – A password?'
In Schnitzler's story there's an exchange of dialogue that was to be seminal for the film. It is dialogue between Fridolin and Albertine, literally translated as follows:

'Oh, if only you all knew!' and again she fell silent.
'If we knew? What do you mean by that?'
With a strange hardness she replied, 'More or less what you're thinking about, my darling.'

['*Ach, wenn ihr wüsstet', und wieder schwieg sie.*
'*Wenn wir wüssten–? Was willst du damit sagen?*'
Mit seltsamer Härte Erwiderte sie: 'Ungefähr, was du dir denkst, mein Lieber.']

This contains crucial elements that we shall find throughout the film: parroting (Fridolin using Albertine's words); a phrase interrupted by silence; slight paranoia; a return to sender ('what I mean is what you're thinking about, take it however you like'). It's as though Albertine were inviting Fridolin to listen to the echo of the words he has just heard.

Kubrick's film retains only the first speech: Alice's 'If you only knew'. It does not have Bill repeat this phrase, but spends more than two hours exploring and developing the spirit of these lines.

'Parroting' is the mechanical repetition of sentences and phrases by someone who does not understand them.[30] Extending the meaning of the word to include people who are supposed to understand what they say, we can say that many characters in *Eyes Wide Shut* display this behaviour.

I have made a (possibly incomplete) list of examples of parroting in *Eyes Wide Shut* and have found forty-six, including examples of what could be termed reverse parroting, when a character repeats what another says, but changes one word:

BILL: Once a doctor, always a doctor.
NICK: Once a doctor, never a doctor.

RED CLOAK: May I have the password, please

SANDOR: My name is Sandor Szavost. I'm Hungarian.
ALICE: My name is Alice Harford. I'm American.

SANDOR: It is as bad as that?
ALICE: As good as that!

The first case of literal parroting is:

GAYLE: Where the rainbow ends.
BILL: Where the rainbow ends?

The procedure becomes systematic when Bill and Alice are talking under the influence of cannabis, the following example being one of six:

BILL: What did he want?
ALICE: What did he want? Oh … What did he want.

There is no parroting in the serious scene with Marion; however it begins again when Domino accosts Bill in the street:

DOMINO: Come inside with me?
BILL: Come inside with you?

Parroting becomes rarer in the scene with Nick, then returns at Rainbow and is also found during Bill's appearance before the 'tribunal' of the Somerton orgy participants:

The mysterious woman,
ready to 'redeem' Bill

Bill and the desk clerk at the
Hotel Jason

MILICH: He moved to Chicago.
BILL: He moved to Chicago?

RED CLOAK: The password for the House.
BILL: The password for the house?

MYSTERIOUS WOMAN: I'm ready to redeem him.
RED CLOAK: You are ready to redeem him?

There follows another pause in parroting, when Bill returns to Alice, who tells him her dream. It begins again in the various scenes of Bill's 'investigation' and his dialogue with the waitress at Gillespie's and the clerk at the Hotel Jason:

CLERK: Mr Nightingale has already checked out.
BILL: He checked out?

There is absolutely no parroting during the following scenes, particularly the one showing the family together in the evening, but it makes a full comeback in the scene of Bill's flirtation with Sally, where we encounter it six times:

BILL: Do you have any idea?
SALLY: I have no idea.
BILL: You have no idea?

BILL: You have no idea?

Leading to the devastating revelation:

SALLY: HIV positive.
BILL: HIV positive?

Parroting is used again at the hospital to confirm Amanda's death:

BILL: Curran. Amanda Curran.
RECEPTIONIST: C-U-R-R-A-N? Miss Amanda Curran.

And at Ziegler's:

ZIEGLER: I had you followed.
BILL: You had me followed?

Lastly, in the final scene between the couple:

BILL: What do you think we should do?
ALICE: What do I think we should do?

BILL: Forever?
ALICE: Forever?
BILL: Forever.

These repetitions, which, in the film are spoken by Bill Harford twice out of every three times, occur in life in all kinds of situations (commercial feedback, checking or confirmation of communication, banter full of sexual innuendo, surprise, the need to make time to think and so on) and are the opposite of wit, the verbal ping-pong which, according to Raphael, Kubrick wanted to avoid at all costs. The characters in *Eyes Wide Shut* are not witty and seldom try to appear so. Every now and then one of them may make a slight gesture in that direction with some kind of joke (Ziegler saying he could recognise his osteopath's skill from the size of his bill) and, at the beginning, the three examples of reverse parroting mentioned above generate a form of 'minimalist' humour that disappears from the rest of the film.

The instances of parroting have several functions.

They transform a particular phrase spoken by an individual at a particular moment into a set phrase, a hidden code; they make it resonate. Yet they also remind us that these words belong to everybody, and that what we say is constantly taken from us, even and above all when we say 'I', because everyone says 'I'.

They often introduce an expectation, bring into being a kind of space between the people who are conversing. They change the sense of time: we no longer know when this game of echoes began, and who said what first. Parroting seems to make it possible to be infinitely indecisive and to hold off the moment of decision: the moment when everything definitively changes, when that which can never be repaired will be committed.

It is also superimposed on the mental echo that occurs in the audience's head when they hear a phrase; it is heard at the same time as that phrase resounds in us, drawing us in in a disturbing way.

But it also reminds us of the literality of speech. It emphasises that language is not thought, it is words, a succession of words. Through spoken language, through prose, it reminds us that all this is a matter of signifiers. It shows us the reflection of another possible meaning to any given phrase, or a hypothetical intention in the phrase (repeating another's words can amount to returning that person's words with the implication: 'What do these words mean that you're not saying?')

Lastly, and above all, it may contain several of these meanings and effects at one and the same time: we can at once repeat a phrase to give ourselves time to think about it (delay), to confirm that we have really heard it (feedback), to steal the other person's words (appropriation) and to create an impression of some kind of suspicion (what else did you mean in saying this?) and so on. It is the shimmering of the signifier in itself, without recourse to any kind of wordplay.

Lastly it embodies the function of the 'password': words are exchanged whose meaning does not matter, and open doors, or try to open them.

29. 'But you know that, don't you?'

In a work of cinema, a closed object, everything holds together, everything goes together. It is because there are about forty examples of parroting similar to those we have revealed that two contrary cases – which we shall call 'delayed parroting' and 'negative parroting' – acquire so much meaning.

An example of 'delayed parroting' is provided by the phrase 'you know that, don't you?' which we hear Bill say to Mandy, whom he has just brought out of her drug-induced coma. He tells her that she cannot go on living like that and must go into rehab: 'But you know that, don't you?'

This boomerang phrase, which in itself means that the other is already aware of what one is saying, comes back to Bill one and a half hours later, said back to him by Ziegler, who witnessed the earlier scene. In this new context as 'delayed echo' it is given an important place, being the last phrase to be heard in this scene, before Bill returns home and

BILL: But you know that, don't you?

ZIEGLER: But you know that, don't you?

finds the mask lying next to his sleeping wife. 'Life goes on. It always does. Until it doesn't. But you know that, don't you?' At the start of Tarkovsky's *Sacrifice* (1986), a father is speaking to his son, who can't reply, as he has a plaster on his neck. The father talks and talks and talks, and knows he's doing it, even bitterly quoting Hamlet's 'words, words, words' (Act II, Scene 2); his torrent of speech conveys an apparently pedantic reminder of the first sentence of St John's gospel: 'In the beginning was the Word'. The little boy plays as he talks, silent, apparently indifferent, not paying any attention. Yet at the end of the film, when it is the father's turn to fall silent because he has vowed to do so and has been taken away as a madman, we see the little boy, all alone now, lying against a tree, looking at the sky and uttering the first words to leave his lips: 'In the beginning was the Word. Why, Dad?'

In theory we can only successfully pass on that which is not self-evident, which we have ourselves had passed on to us. But in the case of *Eyes Wide Shut* the 'father' uses what the 'son' has said, serving it up to him as supreme, minimal wisdom.

It is like Virgil saying to Dante, whom he thus liberates and raises to the ranks of adulthood,

Expect no longer words or signs from me
Now is your will upright, wholesome and free

and not to heed its pleasure would be wrong.[31]
[*Non aspettar mio dir piu ne mio cenno;*
libero, dritto e sano è tuo arbitrio,
e fallo fora non fare a suo senno.]

The father repeats a phrase spoken by the son, passing it round in a circle, as happens in tales of time travel. The 'password' to life literally has no content. 'That' is a word open to infinity; it can contain everything.

In life there is no signified, there are only signifiers.

30. 'Grateful'

The second case of parroting is a case of 'negative parroting': we might expect a word to be immediately repeated by the person hearing it, and it is not. Negative parroting obviously has no meaning unless the audience has been primed and conditioned like one of Pavlov's dogs to respond to parroting.

Let us imagine, arbitrarily, that, like some paintings, a great work is a network of lines which all meet at a single point – where in the work would this point be? We should choose the brief reverse close-up of Bill Harford in the last scene, when he and we have just heard the word uttered by Alice.

To Bill's apparently sheepish question in the toy shop: 'What should we do?' she has answered, taking her time, 'I think we should be … [silence] grateful'.

This is an unexpected word, because up until now the aspect of debt has never been mentioned.

At this moment, in a film in which dozens of lines are repeated word for word, we are shown Bill, who has just received the impact of this word. Bill might be expected to repeat this extraordinary adjective – a real theatrical coup – with amazement, or at least in the form of a question. In the reverse shot of Tom Cruise's face, Kubrick gives him the space and time to do it. But Bill says nothing, reveals nothing, doesn't act in any way; he doesn't repeat the word 'grateful' and the word echoes in our heads all the better than the words that actually were repeated have already done, to the point where we no longer knew who was copying or quoting whom.

ALICE: We should be *grateful*

BILL: …

It is then that Alice repeats the word 'grateful' a second time, as though answering an invisible, unspoken question, and when she does so she seems to be answering this silent, questioning echo that has just been sent to her by the shot of Bill and which is also in our minds.

It would be a mistake to say that Bill is passive here, content to be taught a lesson like a naughty schoolboy. In reality he chooses to remain silent. Sometimes the best words are those we do not say, which allow the other person to take things further. In fact it may be that Alice – who seems really to be thinking about what she is saying and not to know in advance what she is going to say – would not have found what comes next if her husband had immediately appropriated the word 'grateful'. So he has enabled her to speak, and it was the right thing to do.

It would seem that the point of the many repetitions that we have noted is to lead to this moment, to a word that is not spoken, restoring their meaning to all those words that are spoken.

An unspoken word is of course not the same as the negation of that word. Sometimes, in a particular context, it is the symbolic embodiment, the acknowledgment of that word.

Here it comes in the context of what we might call, if not a happy end, at least a 'not-unhappy end'.

31. 'We've managed to survive'

Unlike many films, in which we are glad when things go wrong – something that's been known to happen with art since Aristotle's day – in *Eyes Wide Shut* we are invited to be glad that nothing serious or unavoidable has happened to our heroes. We can be glad also that Bill does not belong to the category of important people, since it is perhaps because he is a nobody that he comes out unscathed. Like Nick, who has gone home with no more than a contusion and is now 'banging Mrs Nick', Bill will end up 'at home, banging Mrs Bill'.[32]

This may not be an elegant way to put it, but it is perhaps a fine prospect, and it's the way life is.

'Lucky to be alive': Bill in Skarkey's Café

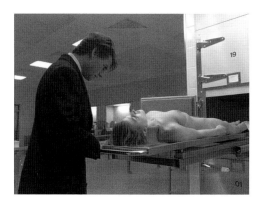

Bill at the morgue, standing over a corpse with no trace of injury

During World War I, between 1914 and 1918, millions and millions of men died or were mutilated in mind and body, not for a cause of liberty or dignity, but to satisfy a few people's taste for glory and grandeur. This is what Kubrick is talking about in *Paths of Glory*. Curiously, this theme of the stupidity of pointless deaths is not the lesson we take from his films, in relation to which words such as cynicism or pessimism have often been written. Some would even like to provide a 'Nietzschean' reading of Kubrick.

Eyes Wide Shut says nothing different from *Paths of Glory*: it is better to live than to put one's life in danger without good cause.

As usual, this message is writ large in the film and no one sees it; it is seen as ironic: 'Lucky to be alive'. Bill should be glad he is alive and we should be glad he is alive, and Alice too should be glad that they are still together 'hopefully for a long time to come'.

It is moreover strange to see that Kubrick often likes to put a minimalist moral at the end of his films, spoken by a character, a narrator, a title or a song.

'We'll meet again' sang a voice over the conflagrations of atomic bombs. 'Its purpose is a total mystery' were the last words spoken (and valid for the film as a whole) in *2001* by a human voice. 'I was cured' says Malcolm McDowell/Alex at the end of *A Clockwork Orange*.

In *Barry Lyndon* it is a title – and not the sententious voice of the narrator which we hear throughout the rest of the film – that gives the final

The end of *Full Metal Jacket*

moral of an 'Epilogue': 'It was in the reign of George III that the aforesaid personages lived and quarrelled. Good or bad, handsome and ugly, rich or poor, they are all equal now.'

At the end of *Full Metal Jacket*, Kubrick's penultimate film, in appearance so different from *Eyes Wide Shut*, the voice of the 'joker' (Matthew Modine) says: 'I am still in a world of shit, yes, but I am alive. And I am not afraid.'

These phrases, heard spoken by a character on screen or by a narrator, or in a song, are often regarded as 'ironic', contemptuous, reinforcing the pessimism attributed to the film. Yet what is interesting is not only the moral often expressed in these remarks ('We're alive, and that's something in itself'), but also the fact that Kubrick wants this 'moral' to be spoken literally, in clear words, rather than being implicitly understood by the audience.

This allows the image to retain all its mysterious quality. If something is said over it in a kind of caption, the image above the title is affirmed all the more strongly as being irreducible to words.

32. 'You will kindly remove your mask'

The moral might be a way of saying, everything that happens to human beings is human and depends largely on human beings: there is neither God nor Devil, nor terrible, castrating Mother, nor crushing Father. All are human.

The character of Nick with his goatee, beautifully adopted by Todd Field, is sometimes compared to the devil, the great tempter, particularly in the scene at the Sonata Café, where he is lit from below. Yet Nick is also a man with four children and a wife to feed in a West Coast city. He is the talkative, weak, human intermediary of the world of the night, like Papageno the bird-catcher in *The Magic Flute*. The comparison with Shikaneder and Mozart's opera springs naturally to mind because of the nocturnal, occult nature of part of the film and the theme of a secret society. Yet here Bill, who corresponds to Prince Tamino, is neither an initiate, nor a prince; he's just another human being like the rest of us, and what's more, he is already married. He is not a hero, in fact there are no

NICK: but never, never anything like this

ZIEGLER: that's a hell of a lot less than he deserves

heroes, only human beings; there are neither harpies nor goddesses, just real, individual women.

The film also talks about the myth that truth is already close to us, 'under a mask', such as the mask of the image. We desperately try to remove the mask, certain that the truth lies underneath. The particular relationship the film establishes between what is said and what is shown (the one neither confirming nor denying the other) has the effect of making the image, and particularly the other person's face in the image, appear as a mask behind which a truth is concealed and which the mask hides from others or from itself. At one point in *Eyes Wide Shut* the main character wears a mask that hides his features – yet when he takes it off we do no not see any more. The idea that we can 'read faces', detecting what is going on inside a person through their facial expressions and behaviour, or the inflections of their voice, is a modern myth, created first by cinema and then by television. *Eyes Wide Shut* offers a critique of this myth.

In the 'great explanatory scene' in the billiard room, ultimately, after several minutes, we have no reason to think that the masks have fallen. Ziegler becomes friendly and familiar at the end, but then he was friendly and familiar at the beginning, when he had not yet said what he had to say. We still do not know whether his friendliness is false or real, and we will never know. It still may or may not be either 'hiding' something or sincere. The masks (over behaviour and faces) are hiding nothing; we must get on with what we are told and what is done. This is perhaps the message of *Eyes Wide Shut*.

Fair enough: people do what they do and say what they say, there's nothing more to find out. Yet, all the same, might we not know their motives and, if these motives exist, might they give us the 'hidden meaning' whose presence we sense?

Eyes Wide Shut tells us that motives do not matter and that we cannot know them.

The characters act in accordance with certain rules of courtesy and decency, but we do not know if they are motivated by a sense of morality or social routine, a concern for appearances, habits or education, the fear of giving a negative image of themselves and so on. Do they know themselves? Bill insists on paying the prostitute he has not gone to bed with, on enquiring after the woman who has offered to 'redeem' him. Sally tells him that Domino appreciated Bill's delicacy where she was concerned. What was it that she appreciated? The money or the gesture that went with it? We must accept that what we give can touch others because of something that we did not intend. It is what we say and do that leaves a trace; all the rest – motives, secret reasons – no longer matters.

33. 'I do … love you'

Nor do we have any reason to say that Alice, who stays with her husband in the end (but does not want to know about the distant future), does so as a result of moral convictions which could be described as fidelity, marriage, a respect for one's given word and so on. When she shows Szavost her wedding ring ('Because … I'm married') as a reason preventing her from seeing him again, it is with an ironic, challenging expression which might suggest to us that he is not to her liking and that her position as a married woman is a handy reason to spurn him. Isn't it the pleasure of knowing that she is still attractive – although her husband no longer looks at her – and of having the power to refuse? Moreover later we see her laughing at the memory of this man, with a laugh that suggests that she found him ridiculous.

Perhaps she was also hoping that he would be more romantic in his attempt to seduce her. But Sandor Szavost does not talk of love in the long term; he quotes Ovid's *Art of Love* rather than *Tristan and Isolde*; he presents himself as an exponent of the *carpe diem* approach ('he also had a good time first', he says of Ovid). He is not promising eternal love or romance; he wants to go to bed right now: 'sex, upstairs, then and there'.

At the end Alice makes no general speeches to her husband, she does not moralise at him; she says, 'I do … love you.'

In this moving last image Nicole Kidman, who seems to look into herself, beyond her glasses – which she is wearing outside the home for the first time – to find what she says, looks very much like the sweet, kind grandmother she may well one day become. Loving and indulgent, she is

What does a woman think about? Alice watches her husband remember the dream in which she 'was fucking other men'

filmed from a slightly low angle and, as in other scenes, we note that she is taller than her husband.

'I do … love you.' This is all we can know: the question of knowing whether she 'really thinks what she says' or whether she 'really says what she thinks' is irrelevant. The film sets up no complicity between what the characters are supposed to 'think' and 'feel', what they say and what we see. The sounds and images create atmospheres, but do not translate or express their inner states. We see people's behaviour, people's faces, but not their emotions; we hear what they say, not what they think.

Kubrick could have made a film in which the characters' 'mental images' or feelings were 'mixed in' with images of reality; and the same with sounds, preventing us from telling them apart clearly. He preferred to use a precisely defined code (black and white for the imaginary scenes, echoes for remembered phrases) which draws a strict line between them.

34. 'Where exactly are we going … exactly?'

There is still the question of the Law, of moral prohibitions, which are more than simply social. Thus Ziegler is not afraid to let Bill see that he was breaking the Seventh Commandment during his Christmas party, and does not bother to justify himself for a second. No character pronounces any moral judgments. The one who does and who calls his daughter a whore – Milich the costume-hire man – later appears as a hypocritical pervert who prostitutes his daughter.

At the same time he is the one who pronounces the Law, who utters a few prohibitions – because someone has to say them. As in the work of David Lynch, there does have to be someone to lay down the law, and if that someone seems to be a bandit (Dennis Hopper in *Blue Velvet*) or a gangster (Robert Loggia in *Lost Highway*, 1996), at least he has spoken. The identity of the speaker changes nothing of what is said.

This film describes a society in which almost everything is permitted when it comes to the depiction of sex, in which bisexuality, homosexuality and the public representation of human nakedness and the sexual act,

The married couple's bedroom

The world outside

whether simulated or not, are tolerated. It is a society in which religion no longer has any power over private life. For some members of this society, social taboos and rules of behaviour no longer forbid what is called 'living out your fantasies', while being unfaithful to one's wife or husband is no longer something that requires an apology on moral grounds. All the same individuals in the West have the feeling that they are no 'freer' than before and that 'living out all one's fantasies' (as suggested in advertisements and films) cannot get them very far. So they are left with the same problems as before.

This society in which 'permissiveness' reigns is, we should note, exactly the same society as the one Schnitzler described in the early twentieth century, a clear proof that indeed nothing much has changed.

The most important values, those in which we can take refuge, seem to be those of sincerity and lucidity. Apparently Alice would find it easier to accept Bill's going to bed with the two models than his hypocrisy when he denies having wanted to do so, since she gets annoyed that he cannot give the question a 'straight fucking answer'. At the same time the film shows that such frankness is no easy task: What's the point of telling each other 'everything' (if it's possible to 'tell everything' …) if it entails the risk of splitting up … At the end of the film, Alice, who has the task of sounding the last note, does not say, 'we are better', but 'we are more awake', echoing the film's title with its oxymoron.

So after the end of the film, if there is a future, the characters are going to make love. Perhaps another human being will be born of this act. In the space between beginning and end a man and a woman have died. But for this hypothetical new human being, who would never have been born had Bill and Alice's adventure unfolded in another way, life will present itself as a new adventure, a path of light always drawing us on, even beyond our awakened vision, to another infinite country.

'Where are we going exactly?' Bill asks one of the two models and she replies, 'Where the rainbow ends.' Bill wants to know in advance where that is and the woman says, 'Well, let's find out.'

Notes

1 Arthur Schnitzler, *Dream Story*, trans. By J. M. Q. Davies, with an introduction by Frederic Raphael (1926; Harmondsworth: Penguin, 1999).

2 'Before me, when I jump into my bed.' This is exactly what the little girl does at this point in the action. Everything in the film to do with Helena is thus stripped of any imaginary dimension: she is as normal and anonymous as can be.

3 See interview by Yann Tobin and Laurent Verchand, *Positif* no. 464, October 1999, pp. 41–4.

4 A 'rhapsody' is a piece of celebratory music, or a piece of no definite form. Neither definition really applies to Schnitzler's story, which is highly structured and has nothing of the epic about it.

5 *Positif* no. 464, p. 43.

6 This of course recalls the 'astral foetus' at the end of *2001*, which is clearly male and is born, we might say, of the Holy Spirit, and indeed from the body of an old man! The child that will be born in *Eyes Wide Shut* will be conceived by a fleshly, human couple – a mortal man and woman – and will, like them, be mortal.

7 Frederic Raphael, *Eyes Wide Open: A Memoir of Stanley Kubrick and 'Eyes Wide Shut'* (1999; London: Orion, 2000).

8 An untranslatable German word conveying an idea of intimacy, comfort and pleasure.

9 Raphael, *Eyes Wide Open*, p. 39.

10 In Ingmar Bergman's *Persona* (1966), one of the most 'influential' films in the entire history of cinema (it has many echoes in the work of David Lynch), the nurse, played by Bibi Andersson, relates an orgy in great detail, without any 'illustration' of her words in images: the only images shown are those of her face as she tells the story and the face of the woman listening.

11 Raphael, *Eyes Wide Open*, p. 85.

12 Ibid., p. 59.

13 *Pulp Fiction* also contains a story that is told but not visualised in the story of the watch.

14 And also Joseph Losey and Luchino Visconti, in films which were never made.

15 In the documentary *Stanley Kubrick: A Life in Pictures* (Jan Harlan, 2001).

16 Interview by Michael Henry in *Positif* no. 463, September 1999, pp. 16–20.

17 Once too much in our view, the superfluous repetition occurring, we feel, at Sharkey's Café, when Bill reads the article in the *New York Post*.

18 On 'rhyme' see Chion, *Kubrick's Cinema Odyssey*, trans. by Claudia Gorbman (London: BFI, 2001), pp.140ff.

19 Tarkovsky, *Time within Time: The Diaries 1970–1986*, trans. by Kitty Hunter-Blair (London: Faber and Faber, 1994).

20 As confirmed in the exchange between Alice and her husband: 'Do you know anyone here?' – 'Not a soul.'

21 The arithmetic exercise Alice gets little Helena to do is a comparison ('subtraction') between the money belonging to two men: 'Joe has how much more money than Mike?'

22 Kubrick precisely refuses to have Bill interrupted at that moment by another character, which is what happens to the character in Schnitzler's story.

23 When Bill appears before the assembled participants, the masked man in the three-cornered hat is seen only at the beginning and does not act; he becomes one mask among many.

24 On the subject of Christmas presents see Chion, *Kubrick's Cinema Odyssey*, pp. 168–9.

25 Although at the end of the film Helena does make a reference to Santa Claus.

26 See Chion, *Audio-vision: Sound on Screen*, trans. by Claudia Gorbman (New York: Columbia University Press, 1994), p. 16

27 This cut is heralded, after the word 'fuck' has been spoken, by a quick fade to silence on the sound track. Following a classic convention, the ambient sound of the shop, which was very present early in the scene, has become quieter and quieter and, by the time the characters have their final conversation, we almost do not hear it at all.

28 The exceptions are Sally, and of course Milich's very young daughter.

29 See my analysis of this scene in *Kubrick's Cinema Odyssey,* pp. 87–8.

30 Chion's term, translated here as 'parroting', is '*psittacisme*' [editor's note].

31 Dante, *Purgatory*, trans. by Mark Musa (Harmondsworth: Penguin, 1985), canto XXVII, 139–41.

32 This is how Domino the prostitute refers to Bill's wife, from whom he has just received a phone call.

Credits

EYES WIDE SHUT

USA/United Kingdom
1999

Directed by
Stanley Kubrick
Produced by
Stanley Kubrick
Screenplay by
Stanley Kubrick,
Frederic Raphael
Inspired by *Traumnovelle* by
Arthur Schnitzler, published
by S. Fischer Verlag,
Frankfurt, Germany
Lighting Cameraman
Larry Smith
Editor
Nigel Galt
Production Designers
Les Tomkins, Roy Walker
Original Music by
Jocelyn Pook

© Warner Bros.
Production Companies
Warner Bros. presents
a film by Stanley Kubrick
a Pole Star production
Made by Hobby Films Ltd
Executive Producer
Jan Harlan
Co-producer
Brian W. Cook
Production Associate
Michael Doven
Production Accountant
John Trehy
Assistant Accountant
Lara Sargent
Accounts Assistants
Matthew Dalton,
Stella Wycherley
Production Co-ordinator
Kate Garbett
Production Managers
Margaret Adams
2nd Unit:
Lisa Leone
Location Managers
Simon McNair Scott, Angus
More Gordon
Location Research
Manuel Harlan
Location Assistant
Tobin Hughes
Production Assistants
Tracey Crawley
2nd Unit:
Nelson Peña
Assistant to the Director
Leon Vitali

**Assistant to Stanley
Kubrick**
Anthony Frewin
Assistant to Mr Kubrick
Emilio D'Alessandro
Assistants to Ms Kidman
Andrea Doven, Kerry David
First Assistant Director
Brian W. Cook
**Second Assistant
Director**
Adrian Toynton
Third Assistant Directors
Becky Hunt, Rhun Francis
Script Supervisor
Ann Simpson
Casting
Denise Chamian, Leon Vitali
Extras Casting
20-20 Productions Ltd
**2nd Unit
Cinematography**
Patrick Turley, Malik Sayeed,
Arthur Jaffa
Camera Operator
Martin Hume
Focus Pullers
Rawdon Hayne, Nick Penn,
Jason Wrenn
Clapper Loaders
Craig Bloor, Keith Roberts
**2nd Unit Camera
Assistants**
Carlos Omar Guerra,
Jonas Steadman
Camera Grips
William Geddes,
Andy Hopkins

2nd Unit Grip
Donavan C. Lambert
Steadicam Operators
Elizabeth Ziegler,
Peter Cavaciuti
2nd Unit:
Jim C. McConkey
Back Projection
Supervisor
Charles Staffell
Camera Technical
Adviser
Joe Dunton
Translights
Stilled Movie Ltd
Translight Photography
Gerard Maguire
Stills Photography
Manuel Harlan
Digital Visual
Effects/Animation
The Computer Film Co.
London – CFC
Video Co-ordinator
Andrew Haddock
Video Assistant
Martin Ward
Gaffers
Ronnie Phillips,
Paul Toomey
Best Boy
Michael White
Electricians
Ron Emery, Joe Allen,
Shawn White,
Dean Wilkinson
Lighting Equipment
Hi-Liting Ltd, Lee Lighting

Cameras by
Arriflex ARRI
Computer Assistant
Nick Frewin
First Assistant Editor
Melanie Viner Cuneo
Avid Assistant Editor
Claus Wehlisch
Assistant Editor
Claire Ferguson
Supervising Art Director
Kevin Phipps
Art Director
John Fenner
Art Department
Assistants
Samantha Jones,
Kira-Anne Pelican
Original Paintings by
Christiane Kubrick,
Katharina Hobbs
Set Decorators
Terry Wells Jr, Lisa Leone
Draughtspersons
Stephen Dobric,
Jon Billington
Assistant
Draughtsperson
Pippa Rawlinson
Construction Manager
John Maher
Stand-by Carpenter
Roy Hansford
Stand-by Stagehand
Desmond O'Boy
Stand-by Painter
Steve Clark

Stand-by Rigger
Anthony Richards
Production Buyers
Michael King, Jeanne
Vertigan, Sophie Batsford
Property Master
Terry Wells Jr
Chargehand Stand-by
Propman
Jake Wells
Stand-by Propman
John O'Connell
Property Storeman
Ken Bacon
Dressing Propmen
Todd Quattromini,
Gerald O'Connor
Costume Designer
Marit Allen
Costume Supervisor
Nancy Thompson
Wardrobe Mistress
Jacqueline Durran
Venetian Masks
Research
Barbara Del Greco
Evening Wear for
Tom Cruise by
Cerruti
Make-up
Robert McCann
Hair by
Kerry Warn
Titles by
Chapman Beauvais
Title Opticals by
General Screen Enterprises
Music Consultant
Didier de Cottigniers

Music Contractor
Peter Hughes
Soundtrack
'Jazz Suite, Waltz 2' by
Dmitri Shostakovich,
performed by the Royal
Concertgebouw Orchestra,
conducted by Riccardo
Chailly; 'Chanson d'Amour'
by Wayne Shanklin,
performed by the Victor
Silvester Orchestra; 'I'm in
the Mood for Love' by
Jimmy McHugh, Dorothy
Fields, performed by the
Victor Silvester Orchestra;
'Old Fashioned Way' by
Georges Garvarentz,
Charles Aznavour,
performed by the Victor
Silvester Orchestra; 'It Had
to Be You' by Gus Kahn,
Isham Jones, performed by
Tommy Sanderson and The
Sandman; 'When I Fall in
Love' by Victor Young,
Edward Heyman, performed
by the Victor Silvester
Orchestra; 'I Only Have
Eyes for You' by Harry
Warren, Al Dubin,
performed by the Victor
Silvester Orchestra;
'I Got It Bad (And That Ain't
Good)' by Duke Ellington,
Paul Francis Webster,
performed by the Oscar
Peterson Trio; 'Baby Did a
Bad Bad Thing'
by/performed by Chris
Isaak; 'If I Had You' by Ted
Shapiro, Jimmy Campbell,
Reg Connelly, performed by
Roy Gerson; 'Naval Officer'
by Jocelyn Pook, performed
by Jocelyn Pook and Electra
Strings; 'Blame It on My
Youth' by Oscar Levant,
Edward Heyman, performed
by Brad Mehldau;
'Strangers in the Night' by
Bert Kaempfert, Charles
Singleton, Eddie Snyder,
performed by the Peter
Hughes Orchestra; 'Masked
Ball' by Jocelyn Pook,
performed by Jocelyn Pook
and Electra Strings; 'Musica
ricercata II: mesto, rigido a
cerimonale' by György
Ligeti, performed by
Dominic Harlan (piano);
'Migrations' by Jocelyn
Pook, Harvey Brough,
performed by Jocelyn Pook
and the Jocelyn Pook
Ensemble with Manickam
Yogeswaran; 'The Dream'
by Jocelyn Pook, performed
by Jocelyn Pook and Electra
Strings; 'I Want a Boy for
Christmas' by Benjamin
Page, Christopher Kiler,
performed by The Del-Vets;
'Nuages gris' by Franz Liszt,
performed by Dominic
Harlan (piano); 'Requiem
K626, rex tremendae' by
W. A. Mozart, performed by
the Rais Chamber Chorus,
the Berlin Radio Symphony
Orchestra, conducted by
Uwe Gronostay; 'Wien, Du
Stadt meiner Träume' by
Rudolf Sieczynski

Choreographer
Yolande Snaith
Sound Recordist
Edward Tise
**Supervising Sound
Editor**
Paul Conway
Assistant Sound Editor
Iain Eyre
Sound Maintenance
Tony Bell
Re-recording Mixers
Graham V. Hartstone,
Michael A. Carter, Nigel
Galt, Anthony Cleal
Sound Re-recorded at
Deluxe Pinewood Studios
Foley Editor
Becki Ponting
Negative Cutter
Trevor Collins
Medical Adviser
Dr C. J. Scheiner MD, PhD
Journalistic Adviser
Larry Celona
Laboratory Consultant
Chester Eyre
Laboratory Contact
Ian Robinson

**Action Vehicle
Co-ordinator**
Martin Ward
Action Vehicle Mechanic
Tom Watson
Action Vehicles
Dream Cars
Equipment Vehicles
Lays International Ltd
Facility Vehicles
Location Facilities Ltd
Facilities Supervisor
David Jones
Fire Cover
First Unit Fire & Safety Ltd
Secretary
Rachel Hunt
Unit Nurse
Claire Litchfield
Catering
Location Caterers Ltd
Security
Alan Reid
Mobile Phones by
Orange
**Dialect Coach to Ms
Kidman**
Elizabeth Himelstein
With Special Thanks to
John Frieda Inc, the City of
Westminster, the London
Borough of Hackney, the
London Borough of
Islington, the London
Borough of Camden, the
Royal Borough of
Kensington & Chelsea, the
Metropolitan Police, the
Thames Valley Police, the

London Film Commission,
The Luton Hoo Foundation,
the Staff of Hamleys of
London, the Transport
Research Laboratory, the
Chelsea and Westminster
Hospital, the Hatton Garden
Association, the Gower
Street Surgery, the
Nightingale Surgery,
Jonathan Boreham &
Associates, Rover Group,
Pro.P.a.g. And.A Geneva,
Leec Ltd, Compaq
Computers, Hewlett
Packard, Bang & Olufsen

Cast
Tom Cruise
Dr William Harford
Nicole Kidman
Alice Harford
Sydney Pollack
Victor Ziegler
Marie Richardson
Marion
Rade Sherbedgia
Milich
Todd Field
Nick Nightingale
Vinessa Shaw
Domino
Alan Cumming
desk clerk
Sky Dumont
Sandor Szavost
Fay Masterson
Sally
Leelee Sobieski
Milich's daughter

Thomas Gibson
Carl
Madison Eginton
Helena Harford
Jackie Sawiris
Roz
Leslie Lowe
Illona
Peter Benson
bandleader
Michael Doven
Ziegler's secretary
Louise Taylor
Gayle
Stewart Thorndike
Nuala
Randall Paul
Harris
Julienne Davis
Mandy
Lisa Leone
Lisa
Kevin Connealy
Lou Nathanson
Mariana Hewett
Rosa
Dan Rollman
Gavin Perry
Chris Pare
Adam Lias
Christian Clarke
Kyle Whitcombe
rowdy college kids
Gary Goba
naval officer
Florian Windorfer
maître d', Café Sonata
Todo Igawa
Japanese man #1

Eiji Kusuhara
Japanese man #2
Sam Douglas
cab driver
Angus MacInnes
gateman #1
Abigail Good
mysterious woman
Brian W. Cook
tall butler
Leon Vitali
red cloak
Carmela Marner
waitress at Gillespie's
Phil Davies
stalker
Cindy Dolenc
girl at Sharky's
Clark Hayes
hospital receptionist
Treva Etienne
morgue orderly

Colin Angus
Karla Ashley
Kathryn Charman
James DeMaria
Anthony Desergio
Janie Dickens
Laura Fallace
Vanessa Fenton
Georgina Finch
Peter Godwin
Abigail Good
Joanna Heath
Lee Henshaw
Ateeka Poole
Adam Pudney
Sharon Quinn
Ben de Sausmarez
Emma Lou Sharratt
Paul Spelling
Matthew Thompson
Dan Travers
Russell Trigg
Kate Whalin
masked party principals

Dolby Digital/DTS/SDDS
Colour by
DeLuxe London

14,291 feet
158 minutes 48 seconds

Made at Deluxe
Pinewood Studios
and on UK locations in
Norfolk and the Home
Counties
MPAA: 36766

Credits compiled by
Markku Salmi,
BFI Filmographic Unit

Also Published

L'Argent
Kent Jones (1999)

Blade Runner
Scott Bukatman (1997)

Blue Velvet
Michael Atkinson (1997)

Caravaggio
Leo Bersani & Ulysse Dutoit (1999)

Crash
Iain Sinclair (1999)

The Crying Game
Jane Giles (1997)

Dead Man
Jonathan Rosenbaum (2000)

Don't Look Now
Mark Sanderson (1996)

Do the Right Thing
Ed Guerrero (2001)

Easy Rider
Lee Hill (1996)

The Exorcist
Mark Kermode (1997, 2nd edn 1998)

Independence Day
Michael Rogin (1998)

Last Tango in Paris
David Thompson (1998)

Once Upon a Time in America
Adrian Martin (1998)

Pulp Fiction
Dana Polan (2000)

The Right Stuff
Tom Charity (1997)

Saló or The 120 Days of Sodom
Gary Indiana (2000)

Seven
Richard Dyer (1999)

The Silence of the Lambs
Yvonne Tasker (2002)

The Terminator
Sean French (1996)

Thelma & Louise
Marita Sturken (2000)

The Thing
Anne Billson (1997)

The 'Three Colours' Trilogy
Geoff Andrew (1998)

Titanic
David M. Lubin (1999)

Trainspotting
Murray Smith (2002)

The Usual Suspects
Ernest Larsen (2002)

The Wings of the Dove
Robin Wood (1999)

Women on the Verge of a Nervous Breakdown
Peter William Evans (1996)

WR – Mysteries of the Organism
Raymond Durgnat (1999)

BFI MODERN CLASSICS

BFI Modern Classics combine careful research with high-quality writing about contemporary cinema.

If you would like to receive further information about future **BFI Modern Classics** or about other books from BFI Publishing, please fill in your name and address and return this card to us.*

(No stamp required if posted in the UK, Channel Islands, or Isle of Man.)

NAME

ADDRESS

POSTCODE

WHICH **BFI MODERN CLASSIC** DID YOU BUY?

* In USA and Canada, please return your card to:
University of California Press, 2120 Berkeley Way,
Berkeley, CA 94720 USA

BFI Publishing
21 Stephen Street
FREEPOST 7
LONDON
W1E 4AN